Issues
Dev
Economics

Issues in
Development Economics

Editors

Gautam Gupta • Manash Ranjan Gupta
Bhaswar Moitra

Sangam Books

SANGAM BOOKS LIMITED
57 London Fruit Exchange
Brushfield Street
London E1 6EP, U.K.

By arrangement with
Orient Longman Limited
3-6-272 Himayatnagar
Hyderabad 500 029 (A.P.), India

© Orient Longman Limited 2000

Published by
Sangam Books Limited 2000

ISBN 0 86311 727 9

Typeset by
OSDATA, Hyderabad 500 029

Printed in India at
Orion Printers, Hyderabad 500 004

Table of Contents

Introduction

The Department of Economics, Jadavpur University has maintained some continuity in hosting the annual Development Economics conferences. The contributors in these conferences, included many eminent scholars of this country and others. Since the loosely defined branch of Development Economics is one of the fastest growing in the field of economics, it was not long before we were getting contributions that were insightful, rigorous and interesting. It was only a matter of time, therefore, that the idea of presenting some of these in a book form germinated. But books require thematic and structural unity. So we have chosen three themes. They are: labour, dualism and trade. We have brought together some articles under each head. We thank the contributors of these articles (as well as those whose articles we could not accept). The errors, however, are entirely ours.

The first section presents three papers relating to some recent developments in the analysis of economic relations involving labour. The specifics of economic decisions involving the use of labour, its supply and the relations established with the growth of various subsectors were a much discussed, but often less analysed, aspect of economic theory thirty years ago. Labour usually entered economic analysis peripherally in the context of productivity and its measures, demography and population studies, migration models or discussions involving choice of techniques.

The last thirty years have seen considerable theoretical research in the economics of labour. Two factors fuelled this interest. First, it was observed in the advanced industrial economies, that rather than the labour market moving towards more competitive models, newer complexities of structure and contracts were throwing up novel factors determining wage formation, and these required fresh insight and newer forms of analysis. To mention a few, collective bargaining, industry-wise unionization, wage indexation, temporary lay-offs, unemployment insurance, job search, moonlighting and the decision to have children required new theoretical models and empirical investigations. The second source of interest has undoubtedly been the ascendency of Development Economics. Less developed economies present a plethora of labour contracts, both urban and rural. In the urban labour market, industry-wise unionization, the existence of given scaled-pay (where the advancement on the scale depends on the workers' age and length of service rather than productivity), the existence of the unorganised sector, subcontracting, and the presence of factors such as caste or ethnicity in specific trades have driven the market outcome away from the competitive solution. In the rural section, various forms of tenancy, interlinkage between credit and labour, bondedness and migration present a host of problems.

It is natural that the theorist would seek and develop specific models that address such issues. Econometric investigations form a large part of the literature investigating these features. Most models use standard neoclassical tools to provide micro foundations to aggregate outcomes. Where some degree of strategic power could be exercised by one or more agents, game-theoretic models have been used.

Severance pay involves a contract between an employer and a worker wherein the former pays out a compensation in the event the worker is fired. Most models discussing severance pay assume that termination of employment occurs as a consequence of external and unforeseen productivity or market shocks rather than as a response to low productivity of individual workers. These models generally consider severance pay as a part of the wage package that occurs with some element of probability. In that sense, severance is agreed upon by collective bargaining and is supposed to counteract the uncertainty faced by the worker. Saha presents here a paper on severance pay that posits a very different motive on the part of the employer for offering severance pay. In his model the firm offers severance pay in order to actually hike up the wage package, so that the industry wage is bid up (through unionisation, etc.) and the enhanced wage prevents entry of new firms into the market. The wage rate (including severance pay) then raises an entry-barrier. This type of motivation on the part of an employer for providing severance pay is relatively rare in the literature; the closest comparison perhaps is a model by Knoeber, where employers provide extremely lucrative severance pay terms in the employment contracts of senior management personnel in order to discourage hostile takeover bids, by increasing the cost of takeover. Saha uses a game-theoretic model to discuss the levels of severance pay that will in fact deter entry and some of its consequences.

The other paper by Ghosh and Saha delves into the nuances of collective wage bargaining between a monopoly firm and a labour union. The indeterminacy of the bilateral monopoly is resolved by strategic decision-making using a game-theoretic framework. The firm initially chooses the capital stock and the level of employment, based upon which it makes a wage offer. Workers accept this wage and begin work. In the second period the workers form a union and proceed to bargain for a higher wage. Disagreement results in a strike. Workers survive at this time on first-period savings. Finally, another round of negotiations leads either to agreement or disagreement resulting in the permanent closure of the firm. The paper is interesting on two counts. First, most models on collective bargaining involve a one-shot negotiation, but this paper is able to include the impact of a delay. During the delay, the strike imposes costs on both the negotiators. This brings the model closer to reality. Second, there is an attempt here to describe the entire life cycle of a firm. In the beginning there is no labour union and wages are accepted as long as they are higher than outside rates. Workers, however save for a rainy day. Later as a union is formed, strikes may occur and the firm may even shut down. This analysis provides a sense of completeness to the work.

Conventional wisdom held that the services sector exists to provide support to other sectors, mainly the secondary or manufacturing sectors. Therefore the growth of output and employment in the service sector must follow a similar growth in the manufacturing sector. Global experience about the relative growth of these sectors suggested otherwise. It is now widely recognized that the service sector is not bound up through backward and forward linkages with the manufacturing sector and it is possible for the service sector of an economy to grow out of proportion with other sectors. The Indian experience is investigated in a paper by Karar. The paper demonstrates that the service sector has an income elasticity greater than one, and that, increases in specialization result in greater automation. The paper is ambiguous about the difference in incremental labour productivity between the manufacturing and the service sectors. The reader should be warned, however, that the equation used for the empirical estimation of the model is different from the reduced form equation derived in the theoretical model presented in the paper.

Dual economy models occupy a very important place in the theoretical literature on Development Economics. Initially, these models were developed to examine the nature of capital accumulation in the less developed economies. Dualism is defined as the co-existence of disparate forces. The first set of dual economy models consists of an institutionally advanced urban-industrial sector and an institutionally backward rural sector. The classical dual economy models built on the framework developed by Lewis (1953), assumed the existence of surplus labour in the rural sector available at subsistence wage rate. Neo-classical models assumed wage flexibility and full employment. However, both types of models emphasized supply bottlenecks and assumed the presence of demand constraints.

One class of dual economy models (often called structuralist) assumes a supply–demand theory of price determination in agriculture and a mark-up theory of pricing in industry. The industrial sector is assumed to have excess capacity, and the level of output is determined by the demand constraint. These models have often been used by Indian authors to analyse food policies and the public distribution of foodgrains. This research was motivated by the controversy surrounding the success of the public distribution programme of foodgrains by the Government of India. The paper by Gupta included in this volume analyses the effects of a levy on food using a two-sector Rakshit–Taylor structuralist framework. His analysis suggests that the policy of imposing a levy is not desirable because it will either create inflationary pressures within the economy by raising the open-market price of foodgrains, or lower the levels of industrial output and employment or both. The analytical structure of the model is close to that of Das (1987).

The role of technological progress on economic growth is well known. Whether less developed countries (LDCs) can benefit from the import of advanced technologies from developed countries is an important issue and has been adequately addressed in the literature on Development Economics. Theoretical analysis of this question is mainly based on the two-country models of the world economy (often called North–South models). However, the two sector dual economy models of small open economies are also used when the interest of the policy makers lies in comparing sector specific technology transfers. Batra and Lahiri (1987) have an interesting (and pioneering) contribution in this context, which uses a mobile Harris–Todaro framework. The paper by Bhat also claims to be based on the two-sector mobile capital framework, and considers a rural–urban wage gap, but it does not assume a Harris–Todaro type of migration mechanism. Results in the model by Bhat differ from those of Batra and Lahiri. There have been a number of two-sector mobile capital models in the literature on trade and development; and in all these models the rate of interest is determined endogenously. However, in the model by Bhat the rate of interest is exogenous to the system inspite of perfect inter-sectoral mobility of capital. This interesting (acceptable?) assumption is not explained in his paper, and it is responsible for his substantially different results.

In recent times, the focus of research has shifted to the dualism within the urban sector. The coexistence of the formal (organized) and the informal (unorganized) sector in the urban areas of LDCs is now well established in the empirical literature. The recent theoretical models of the dual economies also include an urban informal sector. All the important works are extensions of the two-sector Harris–Todaro model and the informal sector consists of those migrants who are denied employment in the urban formal sector. Otherwise all these models are similar to three-sector competitive general equilibrium models.

The paper by Roy deserves special attention because it does not belong to this set of competitive general equilibrium models. The relationship between the formal sector and the informal sector is viewed as an interlinked credit–product contract using a principal–agent framework, where the formal sector is the principal and the informal sector is the agent. The well-known result usually obtained in such models, that the agent is driven down to his reservation level in equilibrium, is automatically established. Hence, the entire benefit of subsidised credit, given to the informal sector, is extracted by the formal sector. So far as the analytical structure is concerned, Roy's model is very close to that of Gangopadhyay and Sengupta (1987) which analyses the credit–output interlinkage between the agricultural traders and farmers. While in Gangopadhyay and Sengupta the explanation of the interlinkage lies in the credit market imperfection, Roy assumes imperfection in the product market.

The last section deals with questions related to the effect of trade and investment on economic development. The paper by Tamal Datta Chau(huri and Smita Adhikary studies within a general equilibrium framework the effects of creating free trade zones (FTZs). The other three papers adopt a partial equilibrium framework to study questions related to the effect of the entry of foreign firms on the welfare of the host nation.

In their paper, 'The Effects of Creating Free Trade Zones in the Presence of a Binding Foreign Exchange Constraint,' Tamal Datta Chaudhuri and Smita Adhikary study an economy that has a number of features which are fairly common to LDCs: shortage of foreign exchange, inelastic demand for domestic products in foreign markets, and demand constrained production and employment at home. They find that if the creation of FTZs in such an economy leads to an expansion of output and employment then the balance of payments problem is eased as well. In marked contrast, pure demand expansion policies to alleviate unemployment can have the effect of tightening the foreign exchange constraint.

Whereas this paper adopts the now standard non-Walrasian competitive general equilibrium framework, the next three papers use a partial equilibrium framework with imperfect competition among firms. All these papers address an important question: Are import liberalization and direct foreign investment in the national interest?

Joysri Banerji Acharyya, in her paper, 'Gains From Full and Partial Liberalization under Duopoly,' examines the welfare implications of import liberalization under duopoly when there is a single domestic firm and a single potential foreign competitor. Her findings are unequivocal and striking; the welfare impact of liberalization and direct foreign investment depends (i) on the nature of the competition that will emerge in the domestic product market in the post entry period, and (ii) on the relative weights accorded to the interests of the domestic consumers and the domestic producer of the good. Consider the case where the Government gives equal weight to the interests of these two groups. In that case, the Government finds that trade restrictions that impose relative barriers to entry of foreign goods, while at the same time not blocking them off completely, are better than both autarchy and uninhibited free trade except in the extreme case of Bertrand price competition without quantity constraints. Further, a shift to equal-import and *ad valorem* tariff regimes from specific tariff regimes improves welfare and increases the Government's tax revenue.

In a framework that is almost identical, Rajat Acharyya's paper, 'Exit Policy, Post Liberalization Game Between Cost Asymmetric Home and Foreign Firms and Welfare,' considers the effect of the entry of a cost efficient foreign multinational into a domestic market that had hitherto been served by an inefficient monopoly. Two alternative scenarios are studied — in one scenario, labour costs are sunk and do not vary as production changes; in the other, labour costs are variable. In everyday language, the first scenario is the one where firms have an existing labour force that is under-employed but labour retrenchment has prohibitively high costs. Under the second scenario, hiring and firing of labour is freely possible and firms hire exactly the amount of labour they need. The principal conclusion of the paper is that the chance of predation by the foreign firm is lower if the labour costs are sunk than if they are variable as in the former case part of the cost is pre-committed and this gives the domestic firm some advantage.

Sugata Marjit in his paper, 'Strategic Aspects of Overseas Joint Ventures,' looks at the benefits of allowing foreign firms to enter into equity based joint ventures with domestic firms. He provides examples of two cases where this leads to a more equitable outcome than the one that is attainable if such an arrangement were not available. He considers the situation where the two parties have alternative risk perceptions about the project at hand. In that case, allowing equity joint ventures increases the level of investment. Next, he looks at a scenario where a domestic firm has a technology transfer agreement with a foreign firm. He argues that allowing some sort of ownership control to the foreign firm via equity joint ventures will lead to the transfer of more efficient technology.

We hope that the collection of contributions in this volume will offer fresh insights to the scholars of Development Economics.

Department of Economics   Gautam Gupta
Jadavpur University, Calcutta   Manash Ranjan Gupta
                                            Bhaswar Moitra
                                               (Editors)

References

Batra, R.N. and S. Lahiri. (1987). Imported Technology and Urban Employment and the North–South Dialogue. *Journal of Development Economics* 25: 21–32.

Bose, A. (1985). Profit and procurement. Mimeo. Indian Institute of Management, Calcutta.

Das, C. (1987). Food Policy in a Dual Economy. In *Studies in the Macroeconomics of Developing Countries,* ed. M. Rakshit. Delhi: Oxford University Press.

Dasgupta, D. (1988). Procurement price, market price, employment and effective demand. In *Studies in the Macroeconomics of Developing Countries.*

Khalon, A.S. and D.S. Tyagi. (1983). *Agricultural Price Policy in India.* Bombay: Allied Publishers.

Lewis. (1953). *Economic Development with Unlimited Supply of Labour.* Manchester: School of Social and Economic Studies.

Patnaik, P. (1975). Current Inflation in India. *Social Scientist.*

Severance Pay, Wage Effects and Entry Deterrence

Bibhas Saha

1.1   Introduction

Entry deterrence through a third-party contract was first modelled by Aghion and Bolton (1987). Soon after, Dewatripont (1988) introduced the labour union as a third party with whom an incumbent firm writes a contract on wage and capital choice. He showed that if information asymmetry exists between the incumbent firm and the union, then renegotiation-proof wage contracts can generate entry deterrence. In an earlier paper, Dewatripont (1987) discussed the usefulness of severance pay contracts in deterring entry.

In that paper, he also provided a sketch of a model involving severance pay similar to Dewatripont (1988). The idea of entry deterrence through severance pay also finds mention in the survey article of Gilbert (1989). Severance pay and labour contracts, in Dewatripont, facilitate entry deterrence only in the presence of asymmetric information. With complete information, the union as well as the incumbent firm have incentive to renegotiate the terms after entry takes place, therefore pre-entry contracts will not be credible. But if asymmetry of information exists between the contracting parties, then post-entry renegotiation may not be incentive compatible and, therefore, an entry-deterring strategy cannot be pre-committed.

In this paper we will use a different approach to develop a full information model of strategic severance pay. The wage and employment choice of the incumbent firm is explicitly modelled by introducing a union and additionally, it is assumed that the wage rate of the incumbent firm affects the wage rate of the entrant firm through labour market interactions.

At the pre-entry stage, the incumbent firm management (or owner) commits a severance pay to its union. This commitment has two consequences: first, the reservation profit (of the incumbent firm) falls from zero to a negative level, and second, the union which sets wage unilaterally is induced to revise its wage upward. Clearly, the total cost of the incumbent firm rises; but much of it is converted into 'fixed' costs due to the severance pay commitment. Now the entrant is assumed to face a labour market where the existing unions play a role in setting the wage. So the upward wage revision in the incumbent firm may trigger a similar wage increase in the entrant firm. This may deter entry.

The key element here is the ability of the union in the incumbent firm to raise the industry wage (wage effects) significantly, either by being a wage-leader among the unions or by gaining the right (through a legal contract) to enforce equal or comparable wages across all firms in the industry. The introduction of this type of union-induced wage effects is inspired by Williamson (1968).

Williamson observed that a 1950 agreement between a trade union and a multi-employer union in the US bituminous coal industry empowered the union to raise wages in all mines by an equal amount.[1] Subsequently, many small-sized and labour intensive mining companies went out of business. Williamson modelled this case as a collusive agreement between the union and the dominant firms to create barriers to entry. Several theoretical models on trade unions such as Manning (1987), Dowrick (1989) and Holmlund (1993) also provide a rationale for assuming such union behaviour. Manning and Holmlund show, in different settings, that co-operation between two unions may lead to uniform wages. Dowrick allows a wider degree of interactions between unions in rival firms using a conjectural variation approach.

Although we follow Williamson in assigning more power to the incumbent firm union in setting the industry wage, there is an important difference in the present case. In Williamson, the union and incumbent employers *collude* on wages; in our model they *do not collude*. In fact, to highlight their non- cooperation, we have selected a monopoly union model having the union independently set the wage followed by the managers' choice of employment. Further, the decision on severance pay is reserved for the employer, so that the employer is the only strategic decision maker. The union does not share the objective of entry deterrence, although its decision does have a strategic impact.

The main result of the analysis is that so long as there are positive wage effects (in the sense that the incumbent firm union can influence the entrant's wage cost), severance pay can deter entry. The greater the wage effects, the smaller the amount of severance pay needed to deter entry. Naturally, a question arises whether it is optimal for the incumbent firm to offer severance pay. The answer lies in the magnitude of wage effects, time preference and how long the firm enjoys the returns from entry deterrence. If the firm is short-lived, then the wage effect has to be strong and the discount factor also has to be high for entry deterrence. But if the returns from deterrence are long-lived, then modest wage effects also make severance pay commitments worthwhile.

The rest of the paper is organized as follows. Section 1.2 sets out the preliminaries of the model. Section 1.3 presents and explains the main results. The concluding section discusses the empirical relevance and policy implications of the analysis.

1.2 The Model

There are three players—the incumbent firm management (or owners), to be called management in short, the incumbent firm labour union and the entrant firm. The game lasts formally for T periods; but all the important decisions of the players that determine whether entry will take place or not are taken in the very first period (1). There is only one entry threat in the first period. In the remaining periods there is no further threat of entry and the same market arrangement will prevail—duopoly or monopoly—whichever results from period 1. The length of T captures the returns from entry deterrence. If T is very long, then the management enjoys monopoly for a long duration after deterring entry.[2]

In period 1, the entry threat is perceived by the management as well as the union. Prior to period 1, the management enjoyed unthreatened monopoly without severance pay and, accordingly, wage and employment were set, say at w^0 and l^0, respectively. We shall refer to them as base wage and employment respectively.

In the face of entry, the management may adopt a severance pay strategy which can alter wage and employment and the entrant's incentive to enter. The strategy and the sequence of events entailed by it, are described as a number of steps that occur within period 1:

Step 1:　The management announces the severance pay, s.

Step 2:　The union chooses w.

Step 3:　The entrant observes s and w. Then it decides whether to enter or not.

Step 4:　If the entrant does not enter, the management chooses the profit maximizing output, given s and w. But if the entrant enters, the management would either 'fight' through limit pricing or 'accommodate' (as in Cournot or Stackelberg).

Step 5:　If the management fights, the entrant exits and in the second period, the earlier state of monopoly will be regained. The monopoly then continues till the end of period T.

An important aspect of the game is that the severance pay commitment is made only for the first period, because severance pay can play its strategic role only in period 1. From the second period onwards, s is reset at zero and w is also revised. If entry has been deterred, w is reset at w^0. But if entry has been accommodated, then w is revised at the duopoly level.

1.2.1　The incumbent firm management

Let the incumbent firm's output be denoted by x which, for simplicity, is assumed to be produced only by labour. Further, it is assumed that the production technology is constant returns to scale. Thus, the production function is $x = A(l)$. Let us normalize $A = (1)$ and rewrite the production function as $x = l$.

The market demand curve is assumed to be linear: $p = a - x - y$, $x, y^3 \geq 0$, where y is the entrant's output.

The management maximizes profits:

$$\pi_1 = (a - x - y)x - C_1(x)$$

where

$$C_1(x) = wx \quad \text{for } x > x_0,$$

$$= (w - s)x + sx_0 \quad \text{for } x \leq x_0.$$

Maximization of profits gives rise to a labour demand curve that has a parallel, but higher, segment for all $x \le x_0$.

The cost for the incumbent firm can be divided into two parts, wage costs and the severance pay cost, if any. When employment falls below its previous level, it bears a fixed cost in the form of severance pay to all the previously employed workers. In addition to this, a variable cost is borne in the form of 'net' wage payment $(w - s)$, made only to the employed workers. But if employment exceeds the previous (or base) level, all payments to the workers are of the nature of variable costs.

Note that by definition even if the management chooses to exit, it has to make the severance payments to all its workers. This feature underscores the value of commitment and the incumbent firm's ability to convince its incoming rival about its desire to fight entry.

1.2.2 The union

The union in the incumbent firm has N identical members out of which x workers are randomly chosen to work and they receive wx. If $x < x^0$, then $(x^0 - x)$ workers receive s and they may work outside and earn v as the outside wage (or simply enjoy the value of leisure, v). The rest of the workers $(N - x^0)$ work outside and earn v.

The union earns at least Nv and tries to maximize net income u:

$$u = x\,(w - v) + \max\,[s\,(x^0 - x),\,0].$$

The iso-income curves of the union, although convex to the origin, have two segments with a kink at x^0. Figure 1.1 shows how the union's preference changes when the prospect of severance pay arises. The dotted iso-income curve uu_1 represents the case when s is zero. Now if there is a severance pay, the iso-income curve will have a smaller slope and a kink at x^0 as shown by the curve uu_2.

The slope of a typical iso-income curve is

$$w'(x) = -\frac{u}{x^2} \text{ for } x > x^0 \text{ and } w'(x) = -\frac{\left(u - sx^0\right)}{x^2} \text{ for } x \le x^0.$$

The union maximizes u by choosing w from the labour demand curve.

Although the union has the monopoly power in setting the wage, it is constrained by the future labour demand curve that will occur in equilibrium.

Here we impose a consistency condition that the relevant labour demand curve is the one that is generated in the entry deterrence equilibrium: if entry is expected to be deterred (accommodated), then the labour demand curve is the monopoly (duopoly) one. In this sense, the union is far-sighted. The union, while taking the monopoly labour demand curve, does examine whether the resultant wage leads to deterrence or not, but they do not decide on the wage with the objective of deterring entry.[3]

1.2.3 The entrant

The output of the entrant is denoted as y. The entrant wants to maximize

$$\pi_E = (a - x - y)y = C_E(y)$$

where $C_E(y) = c(w)y$ is the cost function. The constant marginal cost, $c(w)$, depends on the wage rate set by the incumbent firm union.

If the incumbent firm union is an important entity in the labour market, it can significantly affect the industry wage which will be faced by the entrant. For example, the union can be a leader in the wage setting process for the whole industry as was the case with the United Mine Workers in the US bituminous coal industry. Alternatively, unions can co-ordinate wage setting, in order to maintain solidarity.[4] We shall see that wage effects of the actions of the existing unions can be crucial in erecting barriers to entry.

Let us postulate that $c(w)$ is of the following from:

$$c(w) = \alpha w + (1 - \alpha)v,$$

where α $(0 \leq \alpha \leq 1)$, is an exogenously given parameter capturing the wage effects shared by the two firms. This parameter is similar to the parameter of 'conjectural variation among unions' in Dowrick (1989) and the 'transmission ratio' in Williamson (1968). Since $v < w$, $c(w) < w$ for $\alpha < 1$. When $\alpha > 0$, we say that there are positive wage effects.

Finally, the entrant does not have any fixed cost as such, but it bears only an insignificantly small entry cost, so that entry is attractive only when strictly positive profits are earned.

1.2.4 Static monopoly pay-offs

Now it would be useful to derive some preliminary expressions. The base (monopoly) employment and wage are

$$x^0 = \frac{a-v}{4}, \quad w^0 = \frac{a+v}{2} \tag{1.1}$$

respectively (with $s = 0$). The wage rate is obtained by maximizing the union's objective function, $u = (w - v)x$, subject to the monopoly labour demand curve $x = (a - w)/2$. The corresponding monopoly profit (for one period) is $\pi_1^0 = (a - v)^2/16$. The union's utility in the monopoly case is $u^0 = (a - v)^2/8$.

1.2.5 Static accommodation pay-offs

Next consider payoffs from accommodating entry. In this case, (again with $s = 0$) the union will choose w according to the duopoly labour demand curve. Assume that the post-entry duopoly is Cournot. Then the wage and outputs per period are

$$w^D = \frac{a + (3 - 2\alpha)v}{2(2 - \alpha)}, \quad x^D = \frac{a - v}{6}, \quad y^D = \frac{(5 - 4\alpha)(a - v)}{6(2 - \alpha)}. \tag{1.2}$$

The resultant (one period) pay-offs are

$$\pi_I^D = \frac{(a-v)^2}{36}, \quad \pi_E^D = \frac{(5-4\alpha)^2 (a-v)^2}{36(2-\alpha)^2}, \quad u^D = N_v + \frac{(a-v)^2}{12(2-\alpha)}. \tag{1.3}$$

It is obvious that the management and the union are both worse off in duopoly.[5]

1.3 Entry Deterrence

The working of the model is as follows. The management sets s such that *ex post* they prefer to fight if entry occurs. But their *ex post* pay-offs are not independent of w which, in turn, is sensitive to s. The wage rate set by the union, must be consistent with the equilibrium outcome. If entry is expected to be deterred, then the union is far-sighted enough to set w according to the monopoly labour demand curve and simultaneously w must create credible barriers to entry. Furthermore, s and w must be individually rational. This means that the management and the union would both be better off by deterring entry.

Thus a (subgame perfect) Nash equilibrium involving entry deterrence is the set of s, w, x and y that satisfy the following inequalities:

$$\pi_I^L(s) \geq \pi_I^D(s) \quad \text{and} \quad \pi_I^L(s) > -sx_0 \quad \text{in period 1} \tag{1.4}$$

$$\pi_I^M(s) + \pi_I^0 \frac{(\delta - \delta^T)}{(1-\delta)} > \pi_I^D \frac{(1-\delta^T)}{(1-\delta)} \tag{1.5}$$

$$w = w(x^M, s) \quad \text{in period 1} \tag{1.6}$$

$$u(s) + u^0 \frac{(\delta - \delta^T)}{(1-\delta)} > u^D \frac{(1-\delta^T)}{(1-\delta)} \tag{1.7}$$

The two inequalities in eqn. (1.4) impose subgame perfectness: first, *ex post* the management must prefer to fight than to accommodate and second, the losses incurred by fighting must be less than the exit costs — sx_0 which is the level of severance commitment. The condition in eqn. (1.5) is to check whether choosing a particular level of s is optimal or not. Instead of incurring a cost to deter entry, the management could share the market and enjoy duopoly profits in both periods. The firm's time preference is given by a discount factor δ eqn. (1.6) which simply states that wage is chosen from the monopoly labour demand curve where a particular level of s has been committed by the management. Eqn. (1.7) suggests that the union must ensure that it is better off under deterrence than under accommodation.

The last constraint is important. If the first period pay-off of the union is so small that subsequent monopoly pay-offs do not compensate it, then the union may choose a wrong wage rate that would destroy the management's threat to fight.

Of the four conditions stated above, the wage equation can be easily determined. The wage condition says that wage will be chosen by the union from the equilibrium labour demand curve.

Lemma 1: If (s, w) arises in a deterrence equilibrium, then $w = w^0 + s$.
Proof: If (s, w) can keep the entrant away, then in equilibrium, once entry is deterred, the management will choose the monopoly output corresponding to (s, w). The monopoly labour demand curve is $x = (a - w + s)/2$ for $x \leq x^0$ and $x = (a-w)/2$ for $x > x^0$. The union's maximization problem yields $w = s + (a + v)/2 = s + w^0$.

The union's wage choice is shown in Figure 1.1. The monopoly labour demand curve DD has two segments. The first segment is higher than, but parallel to the second segment. The vertical distance between the two segments is given by s. The upper segment of the iso-income curve uu_2 is just tangential to the labour demand curve at its upper segment at x_0. Consequently, the wage rises fully by s.[6]

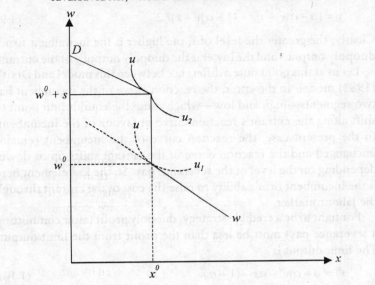

Fig. 1.1

An interesting implication of Lemma 1 is that the incumbent firm's reaction curve, which is based on the net wage cost for all $x \leq x^0$, remains unaffected by the choice of s and w, if that s and w correspond to entry deterrence. Since in the post-entry subgame, the firms are playing Cournot, the management chooses x from its reaction function, which is

$$x = (a - w + s - y)/2 \quad \text{for } x \leq x^0.$$

and $x = (a - w - y)/2 \quad \text{for } x > x^0.$

Note that w is already chosen by the union. So, it is only the level of x that determines whether severance payments are to be made or not. If s and w were expected to deter entry, then by Lemma 1, $w = s + w^0$ and the reaction curve is revised as

$$x = (a - w^0 - y)/2, \tag{1.8}$$

which is same as that without any severance pay commitment. The monopoly level of x corresponds to x^0. Thus the reaction curve of the incumbent firm remains invariant to its severance pay and to subsequent wage revisions.

But the reaction curve of the entrant will be very different because its marginal cost will be higher, causing an inward shift whose magnitude will depend on the level of s.

$$y = \{a - \alpha w^0 - \alpha s - (1 - \alpha)v - x\}/2 \tag{1.9}$$

Clearly, the greater the level of s, the higher is the incumbent firm's duopoly output x and the lower is the duopoly output y of the entrant.

Let us at this point note a difference between this model and Dixit's (1981) model. In the latter, the reaction curve of the incumbent has two segments—high and low—which cause the equilibrium point to shift along the entrant's reaction curve in favour of the incumbent. In the present case, the reaction curve of the incumbent remains unchanged and the reaction curve of the entrant shifts up or down, depending on the level of the severance pay. So the key element here is the incumbent firm's ability to raise the cost of the entrant through the labour market.

For fight to be a credible strategy, duopoly profit (after committing a severance pay) must be less than the profit from the limit output. The limit output is

$$x^L = a - \alpha w^0 - \alpha s - (1 - \alpha)v \tag{1.10}$$

and the corresponding profit of the management is

$$\pi_I^L(s) = (1 - \alpha)\left\{ \alpha s^2 - (1 - \alpha)(a - v)s - \frac{(a - v)^2(2 - \alpha)}{4} \right\}. \tag{1.11}$$

Since $c(w) < w$, $\pi_I^L(s) < 0$ for $x^L \geq x^0$ if $\alpha < 1$. If $x^L < x^0$, then the management chooses x^0 which is its monopoly output.

Had the management changed its mind (after making a severance pay commitment) and accommodated entry, its profit would have been[7]

$$\pi_I^D(s) = \frac{\alpha^2 s^2}{9} - s\frac{(a - v)(9 - 4\alpha^2)}{36} + \frac{(a - v)^2\alpha^2}{36} \tag{1.12}$$

To present a credible threat, the management must choose a level of s at which $\pi_I^L(s)$ must exceed or be equal to $\pi_I^D(s)$.[8] The critical value of s at and above which this threat can be generated is

$$s^* = (a - v)(3 - 2\alpha)/4\alpha \tag{1.13}$$

This is obtained by setting $\pi_I^D(s) = \pi_I^L(s)$ and it can be verified that at s^*, $\pi_I^L(s)$ also exceeds $-sx_0$, the reservation profit.

We shall see that this strategy will result in a remarkably simple case of entry deterrence. Induced by the above level of severance pay (s^*), the union will simply raise its wage by s^* (to $w^0 + s^*$). Through union interactions or labour market mechanisms, wage in the entrant firm also increases.

The effects of wage increases on the reaction curves of the two firms can be easily understood. The incumbent firm's reaction curve remains unchanged because it is based on the net wage cost $-w^0$; but the reaction curve of the entrant shifts down with the commitment of s^* made by the management of the incumbent firm.

An important point is that after the commitment of severance pay, the two reaction curves meet at the incumbent firm's monopoly output level, making entry unattractive and easily deterred. Note that the monopoly level of output $x^0 = \{(a - v)/4\}$ is also the limit output when s^* is the level of severance pay, and it is not sensitive to the degree of wage effects α. The following lemma asserts this point.

Lemma 2: When $s = s^*$, and $\alpha > 0$, the limit output x^L is invariant to α.

Proof: Substitute the expressions of w_0 and s^* in $x^L = \alpha$ and obtain $x^L = (a - v)/4 = x_0$.

The implication of Lemma 2 is that as long as there is some positive degree of union interactions by which the incumbent firm union can raise the entrant firm's wage cost, threats can be made credible. The greater the degree of wage effects, the smaller the level of credible commitment needed as s^* is inversely related to α.

Now let us summarize the important findings in the following proposition.

Proposition 1: i) Let $0 < \alpha \leq 1$ and assume that s^* is chosen by the management. Then entry will always be deterred. The cost of commitment sx_0 is declining in α. ii) If $\alpha = 0$, then entry cannot be deterred.

Proof: i) Follows from the above discussion.
  ii) Set $\alpha = 0$ in eqn. (1.12) and (1.11).

Then $\pi_I^D(s) = -s(a - v)/4$ and $\pi_I^L(s) = -(a - v)^2/2 - s(a - v)$.

Clearly, $\pi p_I^D(s) > \pi_I^L(s)$ for all s. So the threat will not be credible.

In the above scheme of entry deterrence the management not only promises a transfer to the union, but also actually makes this transfer in equilibrium. Interestingly, the promise of severance pay is contingent to retrenchment which does not take place in equilibrium. But still the union receives the transfer via increased wages. The union becomes strictly better off and therefore, will have no incentive to renegotiate *ex post*.

However, the scheme fails if the entrant's costs remain unaffected and the entrant is able to hire from the spot market. This highlights the relevance of labour market interactions. Similar labour practices may be experienced by firms located in proximity (as in the mining or lumber industry), or when firms draw from a common pool of skilled workers (as in the airlines or shipping industry). In other words, unions are able to co-ordinate among themselves in setting wages and other terms when they are in geographical proximity (due to common labour laws and other factors) or when they have common leadership.

One question that naturally arises is whether making such a costly commitment is optimal for the management or not. We shall see that the answer largely depends on how long the monopoly position is protected. If the firm enjoys the monopoly profits for $T-1$ periods, after deterring entry, then clearly the length of T will be critical to justify a given level of commitment.

In the following paragraphs, we examine the optimality of commitment. First, note that the union is clearly better off under this strategy. Its first period payoff increases and then the remaining periods' payoffs are at the base level. So the union benefits from the commitment and it has no incentive to choose a wage rate that facilitates entry. So we need to consider only the management's interest. If the management had accommodated entry, then it would earn π_I^D for T periods. The discounted sum of duopoly profits, denoted by R_I^D, is

$$R_I^D = \pi_I^D \frac{\left(1-\delta^T\right)}{1-\delta} = \frac{(a-v)^2 \cdot \left(1-\delta^T\right)}{36} \frac{}{(1-\delta)}$$

under entry deterrence the discounted sum of profits denoted by R_I is[9]

$$R_I = \pi_I^0 \frac{(\delta - \delta^T)}{(1-\delta)} + \pi_I^L(s)$$

$$= \frac{(a-v)^2}{16} \left\{ 1 - \frac{(3-2\alpha)}{\alpha} + \frac{(\delta-\delta^T)}{(1-\delta)} \right\} \qquad (1.14)$$

Comparing the two payoffs, we obtain the following expression that specifies the critical value of δ (or α) for a given value of δ (or α) for any time horizon T that ensures the optimality of commitment:

$$\frac{5(1-\delta^T)}{9(1-\delta)} \geq \frac{(3-2\alpha)}{\alpha} \qquad (1.15)$$

When T is sufficiently small, say 2, both δ and α have to be sufficiently high. When $\alpha = 1$, the discount factor δ must be at least 4/5. On the other hand, when $\delta = 1$, the degree of wage effect, α, has to be at least 27/28. Clearly, the relationship between α and δ is very tight. For entry deterrence to be optimal, wage effects have to be very strong. However, if T is very long, say T going to infinity, then entry deterrence would be optimal even with weak wage effects, if the discount factor is not too low. If δ is close to 1, then entry deterrence is optimal for any positive value of α. On the other hand, under strongest wage effects ($\alpha = 1$), the minimum value that the discount factor can take is 4/9. In other words, as the returns from entry deterrence increase (with greater T), severance pay commitment would be optimal even with weak wage effects.

Proposition 2:   When $T = 2$, for commitment to be optimal, α and δ must lie in the following intervals: $\alpha \in$ (27/28, 1] and $\delta \in$ (4/5, 1). But when T increases to infinity, these two intervals are enlarged to $\alpha \in$ (0, 1] and $\delta \in$ (4/9, 1) respectively.

We have assumed so far that the post-entry competition between the two firms is output-based and Cournot. This is not a restrictive assumption. Even if the competition is Stackelberg or Bertrand, entry deterrence remains feasible, although the optimality of the commitment may be modified to some extent. Let us now examine two such cases.

1.3.1   The Stackelberg case

If the incumbent firm is a Stackelberg leader in the output market, then it earns a higher profit from accommodating entry than in a Cournot case. So the incentive to take an aggressive stand against entry would be slightly less. However, it turns out that the critical level of severance pay that deters entry is still s^* as given in equation [1.13]. This can be seen from the configuration of the reaction curves of the two firms presented in Figure 1.2. When $s = s^*$ $(3 - 2\alpha)$ $(a - v)$ /4α, the entrant's marginal cost is $c(w) = \alpha$ $(w + s)$ + $(1 - \alpha)$ v and its reaction curve RF_E touches the x (incumbent firm's output) axis at x^0 which is the monopoly output of the incumbent firm. If $s > (<) s^*$, the x – intercept of the entrant's reaction function will be less (greater) than x^0. However, the reaction function of the incumbent firm RF_1 will be invariant to s, as the net marginal cost of this firm is simply w^0.

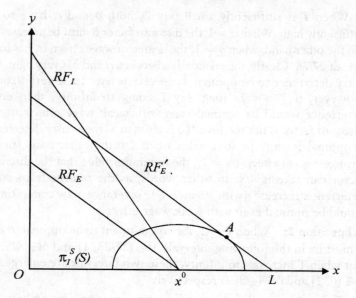

Fig. 1.2

Since RF_1 is entirely above RF_E at s^* and at all $s > s^*$, the monopoly output will be the same as the limit output. It will also be the Stackelberg leader's output. Therefore, the incumbent will not need to set s greater than s^*. If s is set less than s^*, RF_E would shift out to RF'_E. Correspondingly, the limit output will be given by point L and the Stackelberg equilibrium by point A. But the incumbent's profit at the Stackelberg equilibrium will be higher than that at the limit output. This is evident from the fact that the iso-profit curve tangent to RF'_E at point A will always lie below the one which will pass through point L. Therefore, it can be argued that *ex post* the incumbent will prefer to accommodate entry than to fight it. Therefore, the right level of severance pay cannot be less than s^*. Thus, it is the same level of severance pay that deters entry both in the Cournot case as well as the Stackelberg case.

However, the optimality of the severance pay commitment is significantly affected. By accommodating entry, the management earns over T periods:

$$R^{S_I} = \pi_I^S \frac{(1-\delta^T)}{(1-\delta)} = \frac{(a-v)^2}{32} \frac{(1-\delta^T)}{(1-\delta)}$$

whereas by carrying out a fight and deterring entry, it earns

$$R_I = \frac{(a-v)^2}{16}\left(1 - \frac{3-2\alpha}{\alpha} + \frac{\delta - \delta^T}{1-\delta}\right).$$

Comparing the above two equations, the condition for the optimality of commitment is obtained as

$$\frac{2(3-2\alpha)}{\alpha} < \frac{1-\alpha^T}{1-\alpha}. \tag{1.16}$$

An important point is that for commitment to be optimal, the incumbent firm must operate for at least three periods. If T is equal to 2, then the management will not make the commitment. Perhaps this is the most notable difference between the Stackelberg and the Cournot cases. For $T \geq 3$, the suitable ranges of δ and α are also modified. The parameter ranges are slightly reduced for the reason that Stackelberg profits are higher than Cournot profits. Once again with a large T, a smaller wage effect can deter entry. This result is expressed in Proposition 3.

Proposition 3: If $T = 2$, then the severance pay commitment is not optimal. When $T = 3$, for commitment to be optimal, $\delta \in (5/8, 1)$ and $\alpha \in (5/6, 1)$ must hold. As T rises to infinity, the parameter sets enlarge to $\delta \in (1/2, 1)$ and $\alpha \in (0, 1)$.

1.3.2 The Bertrand case

When the post-entry competition is output-based, the entry deterring level of severance pay is s^* (regardless of Cournot or Stackelberg). But if the firms engage in a price competition, then the right level of severance pay is no longer s^*.

As we know, the Bertrand–Nash prices will be equal to their respective marginal costs. The entrant's marginal cost is $c(w) = \alpha(w^0 + s) + (1 - \alpha)v$, while the incumbent firms' marginal cost (net of severance pay) is $w^0 = (a + v)/2$. The incumbent firm's marginal cost must be low enough to drive the entrant away from the market, and that is true if:

$$s \geq \frac{(a-v)}{2}\frac{(1-\alpha)}{\alpha}.$$

Let us call this critical value of s as s^{**}. It can be easily seen that s^{**} is less than s^*. So, deterrence is less costly under price competition.

Further, the incentive to make a commitment is also higher. That is because accommodating entry under Bertrand competition means going out of business. If there is no severance pay, the entrant's MC (due to the particular cost function chosen for the entrant) will always be less than the incumbent firm's MC and, therefore, in Bertrand competition, the incumbent will exit if the entrant enters. So the incumbent firm's management will undertake the commitment only if the discounted pay-offs are non-negative.

1. 4 Conclusion

This paper develops a full information model of entry deterrence through trade union contracts based on severance pay and inter-firm wage correlations. The paper has two merits. First, it has shown that trade union contracts can be credible barriers to entry even in a world of full information. Second, the strategic role of severance pay has been emphasized. An interesting policy conclusion is that institutionally fixed severance pay and public subsidies made to ailing firms in restructuring their workforce can be harmful to the competitiveness of a market. If severance pay is institutionally fixed as in many European countries, then it can facilitate existing firms to erect barriers to entry. In a different vein, Lazear (1990) suspects that institutionally fixed severance pay caused a substantial loss of employment in France.

In many developing countries where economic reforms have been introduced, firms in financial distress may need to retrench workers. The Indian Government has proposed a public fund (called National Renewal Fund) to subsidize severance payments in such firms. If wages are correlated across firms, then this policy can encourage existing firms to use severance pay as a strategy to deter entry.

Unfortunately, there is very little evidence of strategic severance pay. Severance pay, as we generally understand it, is an income-security provision, usually favoured and demanded by the workers. Besides, many countries have legislation with regard to mandatory severance pay. So, for evidence, we first need to look for mutually agreed severance pay contracts between the employer and employees. Oswald (1986) reports a few such contracts from the American auto and tyre industries, but these, are of a risk-sharing variety. In the light of the analysis presented by this paper severance pay contracts may be carefully examined to see whether they support strategic objectives or not.

Notes

1. This refers to the 1965 anti-trust case of *United Mine Workers* (UMW) *v. Pennington* where UMW filed a suit against James M. Pennington et al, owners of the Phillips Brothers Coal Company to recover royalty payments alleged to be due to the UMW as of December 1958, when the company closed down. The outstanding royalty claim was based on the National Bituminous Coal Wage Agreement of 1950, which empowered UMW to raise wages by an equal amount across all firms regardless of technology differences. Pennington filed a cross claim alleging that the National Bituminous Coal Wage Agreement of 1950 was a collusive agreement between the UMW and large mechanized firms to force small and labour-intensive firms to go out of business. The UMW allegedly perceived over-production to be the critical problem of the coal industry. Raising wages was one way of discouraging over-production. Pennington eventually won the case in the Supreme Court.

2. We can give two interpretations of T: First, T can simply be the life-span of the incumbent firm. Second, T can also be the time interval during which the firm faces only one entry threat and that is also in the very first period.

3. Here commitment is made to the previous level of employment. But this does not have to be the case. The incumbent firm can even choose a higher level of employment as the commitment level. In that case, the firm contracts additional workers who may be employed to carry out the threat of over-production. A commitment of this kind was introduced in Saha and Sen (1990).

4. Here I am abstracting from two realistic cases: when the labour union behaves strategically and when managers and union co-operate in setting wage and employment with the objective of deterring entry. The main reason for not considering such cases is to emphasize that the severance pay can have a strategic value even in the most non-cooperative environment.

5. The labour literature cites wage co-ordination in both centralized (at the industry level) and decentralized (at the firm level) systems of wage setting. In public sector units in Europe and many developing countries including India, wages are set through negotiations between the management and a national confederation of unions. In private sector units also, where wage setting is of a more decentralized nature, firm-level unions often co-ordinate within a geographical area or when the unions have allegiance to a common leadership. In either case, wage effects would be strong. Uniform wages also occur when rival firms offer matching wages.

6. Note that the incumbent firm's output and profits are invariant to the degree of wage correlation. As α increases, the reaction curve of the

entrant shifts inward and the union hikes the wage which causes the incumbent firm's reaction curve to shift inward. The simultaneous shifts of the two reaction curves are such that the incumbent firm's output remains unchanged and the entrant's output decreases. Consequently, price increases, but the increased revenue earned by the incumbent firm is transferred to the workers in the form of wages.

7. If the kink occurs just before x_0, then the optimal wage is very close to (or epsilon greater than) $s + w_0$.

8. This can be derived as follows. The outputs of the two firms given by equations (1.8) and (1.9) would be $x = [a - 2 (w - s) + c(w)] /3$ and $y = [a - 2c(w) + w - s] /3$ which will give $p = [a + w - s + c (w)] /3$. Since the resultant x is less than x^0, $\pi^D_I(s)[a - 2(w - s) + c(w)]$ $2/9 - [a - 2 (w - s) + c(w)](w - s)/3 - sx^0$. Writing $w - s = w^0$ and $c(w) = \alpha w^0 + \alpha s + (1 - \alpha)v$, and then substituting the appropriate expressions for w^0 and x^0 from equation (1.1), we obtain the equation (1.12).

9. $\pi^L_I (s)$ initially declines and reaches its bottom at $s' = (1 - \alpha)(a - v) /2\alpha$ and then increases to reach a value of zero at $s'' = (2 - \alpha) (a - v) /2\alpha$. Similarly, $\pi^D_I (s)$ declines from a positive value and reaches zero at $s^\wedge = (a - v) \{9 - 4\alpha^2 - 3(9 - 8\alpha^2)^{1/2}\}/8\alpha^2$. Further, $\pi^D_I (s)$ attains its lowest (negative) value at $s\sim = (a - v)(9 - 4\alpha^2) /8\alpha^2$. It can be easily checked that $s^\wedge < s'' < s\sim$ and $s^\wedge < s^* < s'' < s\sim$ and also lies on the rising portion of the $\pi^L_I (s)$ curve.

References

Aghion, P. and P. Bolton. (1987). Contracts as a barrier to entry. *American Economic Review* 77: 380–401.

Dewatripont, M. (1987). Entry deterrence under trade unions. *European Economic Review* 31: 149–156.

(1988). Commitment through renegotiation-proof contracts with third parties. *The Review of Economic Studies* 55: 377–389.

Dixit, A. (1981). The role of investment in entry deterrence. *The Economic Journal* 90: 95–106.

Dowrick, S. (1989). Union-oligopoly bargaining. *The Economic Journal* 99: 1123–1142.

Gilbert, R. (1989). Mobility Barriers and Value of Incumbency. In *The Handbook of Industrial Organization*, Vol. 1., ed. R. Schmalensee and R. Willig. North-Holland.

Holmlund, B. (1993). Wage setting in private and public sectors in a model with endogenous government behaviour. *European Journal of Political Economy* 9: 149–162.

Lazear, E. (1990). Job-security provisions and employment. *Quarterly Journal of Economics* 699–729.

Manning, A. (1987). Collective bargaining institutions and efficiency: an application of a sequential bargaining model. *European Economic Review* 31: 168–176.

Oswald, A. (1986). Unemployment insurance and labour contracts under asymmetric information: theory and facts. *American Economic Review* 76: 365–377.

Stigler, G.J. (1956). *Trends in Employment in Service Industry.* Princeton: National Bureau of Economic Research, Princeton University Press.

Williamson, O. (1968). Wage rates as a barrier to entry: the Pennington Case in Perspective. *Quarterly Journal of Economics* 82: 85–116.

Strike Threats and Wage Settlements

Saibal Ghosh and Bibhas Saha[*]

2.1 Introduction

In union–management negotiations, workers often back up their wage demands with strike threats. The management or employer of a firm may try to avoid a strike by submitting to the workers' demands if such strikes are likely to reduce profits. A necessary condition, of course, is that it must be optimal for the workers to carry out the threat of strike if their demands are rejected. Several questions are important in this respect : First, if strike threats are sufficient to ensure a favourable wage settlement, why do the workers strike? Secondly, how do workers make strike threats credible, and to what extent is the negotiated wage affected by strike threats? Thirdly, do strike

* The authors would like to thank the seminar participants at Jadavpur University, Calcutta and specially Prof. Amitava Bose, Prof. Debraj Roy, Prof. Abhirup Sarkar, Dr. Bhaswar Moitra, Dr. Anindya Sen, Dr. Ajit Mishra and Dr. Subroto Sarkar for their comments on the earlier draft. The usual disclaimers apply.

threats affect only the allocation of economic surplus or rents, leaving the firm's input choices unchanged?

The first question is addressed in Hayes (1984), Tracy (1987) and many other asymmetric information-based models, where privately informed employers fail to convince the workers about low levels of profits, and therefore, accept strikes in equilibrium. The second question is treated, to some extent, by Lindbeck and Snower (1988) and Kiander (1991). Lindbeck et al. use a full information insider-outsider model under strike and lock-out threats with exogenous strike funds. Their main concern is, however, with the effectiveness of fiscal policy. Kiander endogenizes strike funds, and demonstrates how strike funds counteract lock-out funds in determining wages. In his model, if strike funds dominate lock-out funds (and conversely), then the workers set the wage. But in neither of the models, is bargaining satisfactorily modelled and the effect of strike threats fully analysed. The third question is yet to be addressed in the literature, and is a major concern of this paper.

Whether strike threats cause inefficiency in the hiring and utilization of inputs should be a matter of interest in developing countries. India and most developing countries have policies and labour legislations that are consistent with international norms, and are comparable with those of the developed countries. However, because of the low income base and poor prospects of business in general, tensions arising out of wage negotiations tend to be much greater in developing countries. When strike threats have adverse implications for employment and growth prospects, the tension between wage and profit objectives is reinforced.

The present paper develops a two-period model in the spirit of Lindbeck et al. and Kiander. In the first period, the employer chooses capital and workforce, and the employed workers choose savings to form a strike fund for the second period. It is only in the second period, that the workers can bargain for higher wages and have the option of a strike threat. This paper analyses the choice of capital, workforce and strike fund in the first period, and the bargaining outcomes in the second period.

Second-period bargaining is modelled as a simple Nash bargaining problem; but the threat-points, or the disagreement payoffs of the employer and the workers are determined endogenously by allowing for possible strikes.[1] To be more precise, disagreement pay-offs depend on the consequences of a strike that may follow disagreements. This is, we believe, a satisfactory way of incorporating strike threats into bargaining.

If a strike is potentially costly to the employer because of the fixed cost incurred on idle capital during the strike period, then in the Nash bargaining solution, the employer will agree to a greater wage share and avert the strike. Following this, the employer will try to reduce his future loss from bargaining by under-investing in capital. Employment however, remains at the efficient level. Thus, although strike threats are aimed at extracting a greater share from the organizational rent, they do affect the efficiency of input selection. Therefore, strike threats lead to Pareto inferior outcomes by shifting production from the efficient level.

The under-investment result is similar to that in Grout (1984), and in both cases capital immobility is a crucial factor. However, our result differs from Grout's in two ways. First, capital immobility is not an assumption in our model, as it is in Grout's, but is a consequence of strike. It is commonly observed that during strikes employers fail to move out even raw materials and other easily disposable inputs due to legal restrictions or physical resistance from striking workers. Thus, capital is not by nature immobile or sunk. Secondly, the under-investment result is not robust. If workers' savings[2] are dictated by a credible threat constraint[3] the employer's choice of capital and labour will affect the workers' savings and the length of the strike via the credible threat constraint. Then over-investment is also possible. Employment too deviates from the efficient level.[4]

On the other hand workers' intertemporal consumption pattern gets distorted, although their utility increases. In the absence of strike threats workers borrow in the first period in order to smooth their consumption across the two periods. But if the workers pose a strike threat, and are credit-constrained in the second period, then they must save to sustain the strike. Therefore, the workers will turn from net borrowers to net savers.

The preliminaries of the model and the description of the bargaining game are provided in Section 2.2. Section 2.3 considers the benchmark case of no strike threat. The main results are presented and discussed in Sections 2.4 and 2.5, while Section 2.6 discusses some extensions.

2.2   The Model of Agents' Behaviour

Consider an economy with two employment sectors. In one sector, workers can organise themselves within the firm to negotiate for higher wages and better terms of employment. In the other sector, workers receive a fixed wage determined by labour market conditions. This dichotomy inspired by the insider-outsider literature, is meant to capture the reality of firm-specific unions. Let us call the two sectors organised and unorganised respectively. A typical worker prefers to be hired by the organised sector, as he expects his earnings to be higher, although he can get a job in the unorganised sector with certainty.

2.2.1 The firm

Our attention is on a firm belonging to the organised sector. We assume that the firm enjoys monopoly in its product to allow for some market power of the firm which enables it to get economic surplus. The economic surplus, denoted by a function $Z(.)$, is entirely appropriated by the firm in the first period; but in the second period it is shared with the workers via Nash bargaining. Let the bargaining allocation be given by a function $F(Z(.))$. Then the firm's profits, π, in periods 1 and 2 are, $\pi_1 = Z(.)$ and $\pi_2 = F(Z(.))$ respectively.

The size of the economic surplus is determined by the initial choice of labour, N, and capital, K. Contracts on these two factors are made on a long-term (i.e., two-period) basis. Workers, once hired, are retained for the two periods, due to the costs of firing and hiring,[5] or because of institutionalised job-security. This assumption plays an important role in our model. Capital is assumed to be contracted for use in equal amounts in both periods.[6] This is a simplifying assumption. We can relax it to allow capital to vary between periods, provided that in the second period, capital is contracted before the wage negotiation starts. The reason for this provision will become clear when we discuss the bargaining part.

In the absence of strike or disruption in production, the realised value of the economic surplus will be the same in both periods:

$$Z(.) = R(f(N, K)) - w_0 N - rK, \text{ where } R(.) \text{ is revenue.}$$

The basic wage rate is w_0 and r is the rental rate of capital. Since we need to draw a distinction between $Z(.)$ before and $Z(.)$ after the strike we denote the latter by $Z(s)$, which refers to the surplus after a strike of duration s. The underlying production function $f(.)$ satisfies the following properties:

$$f_N, f_K > 0, f_{NN}, f_{KK} < 0, \text{ and } (f_{NN}f_{KK} - f^2_{NK}) > 0, f(N, 0) = 0 = f(0, K).$$

The firm's problem in the first period is to maximize profits, as expressed in the equation below:

$$\underset{N,K}{Max}\ \pi\,(N,\,K)\ =\ Z(.)+\delta F(Z(.)) \tag{2.1}$$

2.2.2   The workers

There are two possible consumption patterns. If the worker is in the unorganised sector, he earns a fixed income w_0 in each period, and spends the entire amount on consumption. He will neither borrow nor save. If the worker is in the organised sector, then he expects a higher wage (through bargaining) in the second period. Therefore, his consumption depends on firm-specific economic rents.

We consider a group of identical workers who are hired by a monopoly. Each worker maximizes his utility profile over the two periods. The period-wise utility function $U_t = U(c_t)$ is assumed to be smooth and twice differentiable: $U' > 0$, $U'' < 0$. The period-wise consumption depends on the worker's lifetime wage earnings which are w_0 in the first period and $w_0 + v$ in the second period, where v denotes the bargained wage income. As explained earlier, the workers receive a basic wage in the first period, and then in the second period, they enjoy an additional share from the surplus.

The worker's choice of first- and second-period consumption, c_1 and c_2 respectively, is obtained by solving the following problem:

$$\underset{c_1,c_2}{Max}\ \hat{U} = U_1(C_1)+\delta U_2(C_2) \tag{2.2}$$

$$s.\,t. C_1 \leq w_0 - b$$

$$C_2 \leq b\,(1+\rho) + w_2$$

where $b\,(> 0)$ is worker's savings, and δ represents the discount factor $\delta = (1 + \rho)^{-1}$, $1 > \delta > 0^7$ and ρ is the rate of interest on workers' savings.

2.2.3   The wage bargaining process

The second-period bargaining is modelled as a simple Nash bargaining problem. The bargaining takes place between the firm and the workers' union. The union is relevant only in the second period and its objective is assumed to be the maximization of the total wage bill, where, M is the reservation wage bill plus surplus.

$$M = (w_0 + v) N \qquad (2.3)$$

and $vN = Z(.) - F(Z(.))$.

In the Nash solution, the union and the firm share the economic surplus after netting out their respective disagreement pay-offs. We depart from the usual practice of holding the disagreement pay-offs as exogenously fixed. The determination of these pay-offs is explicitly modelled by specifying a course of actions that the agents are free to pursue in the event of a disagreement in bargaining.

2.2.4 The threat points

In the standard case, with no possibility of strike, the union's disagreement pay-off will simply be $w_0 N$, and it will be zero for the firm provided that capital is not sunk. When capital can be easily withdrawn, the firm will close down and avoid loss.

We modify the standard case by allowing the union to call a strike in the event of a disagreement in the first stage of bargaining. During a strike, all production activities are suspended and capital is temporarily sunk. Any settlement reached after the strike, will be based on the remaining organizational rent. The loss already suffered by capital will have to be borne by the employer. It is these post-strike pay-offs which are to be regarded as disagreement pay-offs (or threat points) to the original bargaining game.

2.2.5 The overall game

The game begins in period 1. The firm chooses the level of capital stock and employment, and the workers choose their consumption profiles. These choices may not be simultaneous. In fact the workers' decision should follow the firm's decisions. But these two decisions may not be strategically connected. We consider these decisions with Cournot assumptions. A possible extension would be to consider the case where the decisions are made sequentially so that the firm (or the worker) has a first mover advantage in their choice of variables.

The second period of the game is, for analytical purposes, divided into three sub-stages. In the first sub-stage, the workers form a union, and bargain with the firm over the division of the surplus. If agreement occurs, the second period insider wage gain (v) is determined, and production takes place. Disagreement moves the analysis to the second sub-stage. In the second sub-stage, the union declares a strike of durations s, $(1 > s > 0)$.[8] During the strike, the firm's revenue declines by a proportion θ due to its temporary absence from the market. In general, θ will be a function of strike duration s, i.e. $\theta = \theta(s)$, $\theta'(s) > 0$. Simultaneously, the workers experience an income loss and resort to a subsistence level of consumption c_0, financed out of their first-period savings. Finally, once the strike ends, there is another round of union-firm negotiations. If agreement occurs, the bargained wage is determined, otherwise the firm is closed down for good.

Notice that the two rounds of bargaining are indistinguishable if the strike length is zero, in which case the bargaining game collapses to the standard Nash bargaining game. In other words, the second-period bargaining game is nothing but two rounds of standard Nash bargaining separated by a possible strike.

It will, however, be clear that the last two sub-stages are unlikely to occur in equilibrium, because of perfect information shared by all agents. These sub-stages play a role in determining the disagreement pay-offs. Following the backward induction principle, we first solve the second phase (post-strike) of bargaining, and use the outcome to compute the disagreement points for the original bargaining problem.

2.3   The Case of No Strike Threat

We first consider the case when $s = 0$. Here, we have the standard Nash bargaining problem:

$$\underset{v}{Max}\ (M - Nw_0)(\pi)$$

Using $\pi = [Z(.) - vN]$ and $M = (w_0 + v)N$, we get,

$$v^0 = \frac{Z(N,K)}{2N}$$

Accordingly, the firm's profits and the union's utility are

$$\pi^0 = \frac{Z(N,K)}{2}$$

$$M^0 + (v^0 + w_0)N$$

The firm chooses (N, K) to maximize $\pi^0(N, K)$ and this gives

$$R_N(N, K) = w_0 = 0$$

$$R_K(N, K) - r = 0.$$

as the two first-order conditions of profit maximization. The level of employment and the capital stock are chosen efficiently as their marginal products equal the respective factor prices. The representative worker will choose a negative level of strike fund, which means that the worker, in fact, seeks to smooth consumption through borrowing. This can be shown as follows. The first-order condition for the worker's maximization problem as shown in eqn. (2.2) is given by

$$U_1'(.) - \delta U_2'(.) (1 + \rho) = 0$$

which, on rearrangement yields $c_1 = c_2$.

Since $c_2 = w_0 + v + b(1 + \rho) = w_0 - b = c_1$, b must be negative, $b = -[v/(2 + r)] < 0$. That is, the worker borrows in the first period. So in the absence of a strike threat, consumption will be smooth over two periods.

Proposition 1: With no strike threat, the levels of capital and employment of the firm are at their efficient levels. The representative worker will seek to smooth his intertemporal consumption profile by borrowing in the first period.

2.4 Wage Determination in the Presence of Strike Threats

Strike threats can significantly affect the bargaining outcome, simply by altering the disagreement pay-offs. If the workers have the ability to strike, and subsequently force the employer to concede to a better wage deal, then the workers will refuse all the wage offers that can be improved upon by a strike. Therefore, a natural outcome of bargaining in this case is to settle at a wage that is greater than the post-strike wage rate.

However, several conditions must be satisfied by the workers for their threats to be effective. First, they must have enough savings to sustain a subsistence consumption c_0 during the strike period, since we have assumed away second-period borrowing. This constraint can be called *consumption constraint*. Second, the strike should not be so long as to reduce economic surplus to zero, since it would not be beneficial to the workers. Let us call this the *economic surplus constraint*. Finally, for the threat of strike to be credible, the post-strike pay-off $\hat{M}(s)$, *for the worker must be greater than* M^0, the standard Nash pay-off in the absence of strike threats. But we also expect the workers to realise the gains from strike threats without starting a strike. For this to happen, the equilibrium pay-off of the union from the pre-strike bargaining, $M^*(s)$, must exceed its post-strike pay-off $\hat{M}(s)$. That $M^*(s) > \hat{M}(s)$ is easily satisfied as $\hat{M}(s)$ becomes the disagreement pay-off. The restriction required is: $\hat{M}(s) > M_0$. This restriction is called the *credible threat constraint*. These constraints can be written as:

$s \leq b\,(1+\rho)\,/C_0$ (Consumption constraint);

$Z\,(s) > 0$, (Economic surplus constraint);

$\hat{M}(s) > M_0{}^9$ (Credible threat constraint).

During a strike production is suspended and the movement of goods and materials in and out of the firm is affected. Workers may prevent inventory clearance, or resale and withdrawal of movable capital, essentially to make the employer bear a cost. This cost results in a negative return to capital during the strike. With a strike of duration s, the *net* return on capital is *assumed to be* $sK\sigma$, $\sigma < 0$. If K is fixed capital, then σ can be interpreted as interest liability, or rental payment for the duration of s, which is to be borne entirely by the employer. On the other hand, if K is variable capital, then σ is interpreted as the loss from resale of the 'sK' portion of total capital. In that case, one can write $\sigma = q - r$, where q is the resale price and r is the purchase price of capital, $r > q$. If, however, capital cannot be resold then $\sigma = -r$.

Now, suppose that there is a strike of length s, $1 > s > 0$, which satisfies all the three constraints mentioned above. After the strike, the players meet for another round of bargaining over the surplus $Z(.)$ that has already been affected by s. So the surplus available for bargaining is

$$Z\,(s) = \theta(s)\,R(N,\,K) - (1-s)\,rK - w_0 N$$

Note that, the cost of capital is only a fraction of its total cost, since, consequent upon the strike, capital is employed for $(1-s)$ duration only.[10] Since the spot-market wage is w_0, the union's disagreement pay-off is Nw_0. The firm is assumed to avoid any subsequent loss, so that its disagreement pay-off in this subgame is zero.

The Nash bargaining solution is given by the following problem:

$$\underset{V}{Max}\ (M(s) - Nw_0)(\pi\,(s) - s\sigma K)$$

This gives

$$\hat{v} = \frac{Z(s) - s \sigma K}{2N} \qquad (2.4)$$

The utility and profit levels of the union and the firm are

$$\hat{M}(s) = (\hat{v} + w_0) N \qquad (2.5)$$

$$\pi(s) = \frac{Z(s) + s \sigma K}{2}$$

2.4.1   The bargaining outcome

The original bargaining problem is now redefined in terms of newly obtained disagreement pay-offs, $\hat{M}(s)$ (s) and $\hat{\pi}$ (s).
The Nash bargaining problem is then written as,

$$\underset{v}{Max} \ (M - \hat{M}(s))(\pi - \hat{\pi}(s))$$

This gives

$$V^{\cdot} = [(Z - s \sigma K) / 2N] \qquad (2.6)$$

Therefore, the union's utility and the firm's profits are

$$M^{\cdot} = [(Z - s \sigma K)/2] + w_0 N \qquad (2.7)$$

$$\pi^{\cdot} = [(Z + s \sigma K) / 2]$$

Clearly, an increase in the strike length raises the second-period bargained wage and consequently, the union's overall utility. There are two opposing forces at work: on the one hand is the workers' desire to obtain a larger share of the surplus by sustaining a longer strike duration propelled by higher individual savings and on the other is the firm's desire to concede as low a share of the surplus as possible without risking a strike. A credible strike threat strengthens the workers' bargaining position, getting them a larger share of the surplus and consequently, a higher union utility. The converse is the case for the firm's profits.
Given the expression for s, the strike length, it is clear that,

$$v \ (b) = Z / 2N - [(\sigma K / 2N) \ (b \ (1 + \rho) / C_0]$$

When $s = 0$, $v \ (b; N, K) = (Z/2N)$ — independent of b, so that changes in savings leave the surplus unaffected.
The bargaining part is illustrated in Figure 2.1. In the absence of a strike threat, the bargaining solution is given by point E, at which

the bargaining objective function will be tangential to the bargaining frontier given by the line $Z = M + \pi$. Since the bargaining powers are equal, the symmetric pay-offs will be given by the 45 degree line. The union's payoff would be M_0. This solution is based on the assumption that the disagreement pay-offs are zero for the employer and Nw_0 for the union.

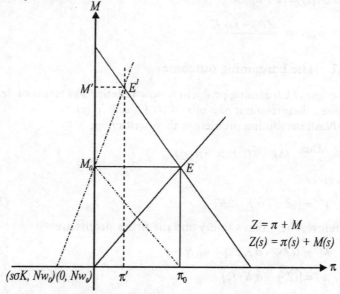

Fig. 2.1   A binding credible threat constraint

However, when the possibility of strike is recognised, point E is no longer the solution. In the post-strike situation, the bargaining frontier shifts inward to $Z(s)$ indicating the reduction of the set of feasible allocations. Moreover, some of the allocations have negative pay-offs for the employer. The disagreement pay-offs in this subgame are $S\sigma K$ for the employer and Nw for the workers. Accordingly, we reach a bargaining solution given by point E" at which the union's pay-off must be at least M_0. This is necessary for the fulfillment of a credible threat constraint. But we also know that is only one of the equilibrium possibilities which will be avoided by the agents in the first place. The solution corresponding to the point E" forms the threat points of the first round of bargaining, and determines the equilibrium allocation. The equilibrium is obtained at E', with pay-offs being (π^*, M^*). Clearly, the union is better off, and the firm worse off in this allocation.

2.5   The First-period Solution

Having determined the wage gain and the sustainable strike duration, we now proceed to analyse the worker's and the firm's decision problem in the first period. Here two alternative possibilities emerge from the constraints on the strike length. The announced duration of the strike will be given by the minimum of the different limits on s implied by the three constraints. For a credible threat constraint, all we need is that $\hat{M}(s)$ is above M^0 at some s. The derivative of $\hat{M}(s)$ is $rK + Z'(s) / 2$, which could be negative or positive depending on the magnitude of $Z'(s)$, $Z'(s) < 0$. Here we assume that $\hat{M}(s)$ is initially increasing, and then declining. Since $\hat{M}(s) = M^0$ at $s = 0$, and $\hat{M}(s) < 0 < M^0$, at $s = 1$, the equality between the two would be restored at some $s = \hat{s} < 1$. So, for the credibility constraint to be satisfied the announced strike length must not exceed $\hat{s}$. Further, the economic surplus constraint — i.e., $Z(s) > 0$ — may be violated at an $s > \hat{s}$, because when $Z(s) = 0$, $\hat{M}(s)$ will be strictly less than M^0. Therefore, the strike duration will be given by the minimum of s dictated by the consumption or credible threat constraint. Hence two alternative possibilities arise. When the strike duration is given by the consumption constraint, the workers choose optimal savings. But when it is otherwise, the workers' savings are fixed by the credible threat constraint.

Case (i): The consumption constraint is binding.   As explained before, we shall confine ourselves to the so-called Cournot case where decisions of the firm have no temporal effect on the workers' savings choice.[11] We substitute the value of b, given by the consumption constraint into the worker's decision problem

$$\underset{b}{Max} \quad U_1[w_0 - b] + \delta\, U_2[b\,(1+\rho) + w_0 + Z / 2N - (1-\phi)\,b]$$

$$\text{where} \quad (1-\phi) = \sigma K(1+\rho)/2NC_0 = \left(\frac{\sigma K}{2}\right)\left(\frac{1}{\delta C_0}\right)$$

Hence ϕ is (one minus) the net cost of capital *adjusted* for the union power, time preference parameter and total subsistence consumption. The first-order condition for an interior maximum gives

$$U_1'(\cdot) / U_2'(\cdot) = \left(1 - \frac{\sigma K}{2 N C_0}\right) \tag{2.8}$$

The firm chooses (N, K) to maximize profits, $\pi(N, K)$, given by

$$\pi(N, K) = \left(1 + \frac{\delta}{2}\right) Z(N, K) + \frac{\delta S\sigma K}{2}$$

First order conditions for an interior optimum yield

$$\left(1 + \frac{\delta}{2}\right)[R_N(\cdot) - w_0] = 0 \tag{2.9}$$

$$\left[\left(1 + \frac{\delta}{2}\right)(R_K(\cdot) - r) + \frac{\delta s\sigma}{2}\right] = 0 \tag{2.10}$$

so that there is under-investment.[12]

The three first-order conditions yield the following conclusions.[13] First, the workers sacrifice consumption smoothing in order to save for the strike fund. Since, $\sigma < 0$, from equation (2.8), $U'_1(.) > U'_2(.)$, implying $C_1 < C_2$. In the contrasting case of no strike threat, workers borrow for the purpose of consumption smoothing. The firm's choice of capital is shown in equation (2.10). Since $\sigma < 0$, marginal product of capital exceeds its price—a case of under-investment. However, the *ex post* marginal product equals the basic wage rate.

Proposition 2: Suppose that the firm's choice of capital stock and employment level has no sequential effect on the workers' savings, then, with strike threats, capital will be under-invested, but employment will be *ex post* efficient. The representative worker will save to sustain the strike threat.

Intuitively, since the bargaining is about the division of the surplus and not about basic wages, the firm has no incentive but to diverge from the optimal employment arrangement. On the other hand, a strike threat causes capital to get 'locked in': the higher the investment, the greater the amount of capital sunk. As a result, the firm's threat-point is considerably reduced. The firm is therefore induced to invest less with a potential strike threat than otherwise.

Case (ii): Strike duration given by the credible threat constraint: In this case, s is given by $\hat{M}(s) = M^0$ which can be written as,

$$R(N, K; s) + s(r - \sigma)K - R(N, K) = 0$$

Let $\hat{s}$ solve this equation. Then b is given by the consumption constraint evaluated at $\hat{s}$. The worker's first-order condition for savings now becomes irrelevant. However, the firm's first order conditions for employment and capital remain unchanged except for the fact that s is set at $\hat{s}$.

The first-order condition for the firm yields

$$N: (1 + \sigma / 2) (R_N (.) - w_0) + (\sigma K / 2) \, \partial \hat{s} \, / \partial N = 0 \qquad (2.12)$$

$$K: (1 + \delta / 2) (R_K(.) - r) + \sigma \, \hat{s} \, / 2 + (\sigma K / 2) \, \partial \hat{s} \, / \partial K = 0$$

Evaluating $\partial s / \partial N$ and $\partial s / \partial K$, we find that

$$\partial s / \partial N = [R_N (.) (1 - \theta(\hat{s})] / [\theta'(\hat{s}) R(N, K) + K (r - \sigma) \qquad (2.13)$$

$$\partial s / \partial K = [R_K (.) (1 - \theta(\hat{s}) - \hat{s} (r - \sigma)] / [\theta'(\hat{s}) R(N, K) + K(r - \sigma)$$

Combining eqn. (2.12) and (2.13) we can make the following observations. Firstly, employment is sub-optimal, optimal or over-optimal according as the partial derivative of the strike length with respect to employment exceeds, equals or falls short of zero. Secondly, if the partial derivative of the strike length with respect to capital exceeds zero, then there is under-investment. Finally, for over-investment to occur, $\partial s / \partial K$ must have a negative sign. It is therefore clear that the under-investment as in Grout (1984) is not robust and that under certain circumstances, over-investment (along with under-employment) is also possible. In a related context, Manning (1987) has shown under what circumstances over-investment can occur in a sequential bargaining framework when the bargaining powers of the agents vary at different stages of the bargain.

2.6   Conclusion

The new result of this paper is that strike threats which aim at redistributing economic surplus, can cause inefficiencies in the allocation of factors. Strikes can be costly to the employer in many ways. We have considered the cost incurred due to the temporary idleness of capital. Since such costs are entirely borne by the employer, in a post-strike settlement, the employer will have a disadvantage *vis-à-vis* the workers. Therefore, the employer will prefer to settle for an outcome which is favourable to the workers, but is also better than his own post-strike pay-off.

Such a distortion is due to the strategic impact of the workers' strike fund on the determination of employment and investment. However, the magnitude and direction of this strategic impact depends on how the strike fund is determined. If the strike fund is determined by optimal savings then capital will be under-invested and employment will be at the *ex post* efficient level. But if the strike fund is dictated by the credible threat constraint and the workers save accordingly, then capital and employment will be inefficiently chosen.

It is to be noted that in this case the employer can protect himself, to some extent, by influencing the strike length through his choice of inputs. In some sense, this allows the employer to have a Stackelberg-like advantage. An interesting extension of this work would be to allow the employer to have a strategic inventory holding to counteract the loss from strike. In that case, the workers' bargaining advantage may be greatly reduced. The overall bargaining outcome may be close to the symmetric partition, but only after having incurred a great deal of dead-weight loss due to the inventory and strike fund. Clearly, one can examine what policies can be effective in reducing the dead-weight loss.

Notes

1. Nash bargaining is not essential for our purpose. A non-cooperative bargaining game could suffice provided that the game recognises the players' disagreement pay-offs. For example, a 'split-the-difference' game will yield similar results, when the gains from trade are calculated after subtracting the disagreement pay-offs.
2. See the Optimisation programme given by (2.3) and page 32.
3. See page 35.
4. That sequencing of decision-making can change the Grout's result, has been illustrated by Manning (1987). He allowed wage and employment to be bargained for sequentially, while the bargaining strength of each party changes between each stage of bargaining. Over-investment occurs under certain conditions.
5. Similar reasons are also made by Lindbeck and Snower (1988), who argued that replacing insiders with low-wage outsiders is usually not profitable to firms because of the high turnover costs associated with the replacement of incumbent workers.
6. Depreciation is ignored.
7. We assume that workers cannot borrow immediately before a strike in the second period as lenders may face substantial risk due to the uncertainty of post-strike settlements. Although information is symmetric and certain between union and employer, outside agents such as lenders may not be sufficiently sure about the success of a strike. Hence, a strike fund can be created only out of the workers' savings or their first period borrowings. We shall, however, see that workers save instead of borrowing in the first period in order to create the strike fund.
8. Our interest lies in the effect of a strike threat and its consequences. Therefore we do not allow for the possibility of lockouts or lockout funds on the part of the firm. A richer model can be developed if we allow lockout funds to counteract strike funds.
9. Note that $M^{\wedge}(s)$ accrues to the union only after time s, following a rejection of the wage offer M^0. Hence, $M^{\wedge}(s)$ should be discounted by

the factor δ^S. However, for simplicity, we have chosen discrete discounting. Pay-offs occurring within the same period, but different in order, are not discounted.

10. There is an asymmetry with returns to the firm and the workers consequent upon a strike threat. This is due to the fact that when a strike is legal, the workers do not lose their strike period wages, in many countries. This can, however, be changed without altering the basic insights of the model.

11. The following explains why the workers do not borrow in the first period to form the strike fund. Let B denote borrowing and b savings. So the workers' problem in the first period is given by the following expression:

$$U_1[w_0 + B - b] + \delta U_2[w_0 + Z/2N - b(1 + \rho) \sigma K/2NC_0 - B(1 + \rho) + b(1 + \rho)$$

First-order conditions for an interior maximum yield

$$B: U'_1(.) + \delta U'_2(.)[-(1 + \rho)] = 0$$

$$b: -u'_1(.) + \delta U'_2(.)(1 - \sigma K/2 N C_0)[1 + \rho] = 0$$

It is clear that the two equations cannot hold simultaneously. So, either $B = 0$ or $b = 0$. When $B = 0$, workers save in the first period so as to earn a higher wage gain in period 2. If, however $b = 0$, workers borrow in period 1 so as to smooth their intertemporal consumption. But then the borrowing would not go into strike funds.

12. It is easy to check that the second-order conditions are satisfied by virtue of the concavity of the revenue function.

13. The first-order conditions form the Nash equilibrium of the period 1 subgame, provided the equilibrium exists. In formal terms, this means that the reaction functions of the firm and the worker must intersect each other at least once. The reaction curves can be obtained from the three first-order conditions. To simplify, assume that $f_{NK}(.) = 0$. Employment is determined entirely by equation (2.9). Then equations (2.8) and (2.10) can be used to show that under weak concavity, the reaction functions $b(K)$ and $K(b)$ have opposite slopes giving rise to the possibility that they intersect in the (b, K) space.

References

Grout, P. (1984). Investment and wages in the absence of binding contracts: a Nash bargaining approach. *Econometrica* 52: 449–460.

Hayes, B. (1984). Unions and strikes with asymmetric information. *Journal of Labor Economics* 2: 57–83.

Kiander, J. (1991). Strike threat and the bargaining power of insiders. *Scandinavian Journal of Economics* 39: 760–784.

Lindback, A. and D. J. Snower. (1988). Strike and lockout threats and fiscal policy. *Oxford Economic Papers* 39: 760–784.

Manning, A. (1987) : An integration of trade union models in a sequential bargaining framework. *The Economic Journal* 97: 212–39.

Oswald, A. J. (1985). The economic theory of trade unions: An introductory survey. *Scandinavian Journal of Economics* 87: 197–225.

Tracy, J. (1987). An empirical test of an asymmetric information of strikes. *Journal of Labor Economics* 5: 149–173.

Employment Growth in the Service Sector in India

Probir Karar

3.1 Introduction

During the last four decades, the composition of economic activities in the Indian economy has changed. The service sector has grown faster than the secondary sector. As a result, the share of the service sector in terms of employment and output in the national employment and GNP has increased substantially over the last 40 years. This paper seeks to explain the phenomenal growth of employment in the services sector *vis-à-vis* the secondary sector.

The theoretical model is based on the lines proposed by Baumol (1967).[1] It is a simple two-sector macroeconomic model with a differential growth in labour productivity. Fuchs (1985)[2] documented the emerging role of the service sector in the U.S. economy and then offered and tested three hypotheses for the relative growth of employment in the service sector.[3]

Against this theoretical background, this paper seeks to test Fuchs' hypotheses in the context of the Indian economy to explain the relative growth of employment in the service sector.

Sections 3.2 and 3.3 highlight the theoretical framework of the model and present the empirical results. The final section concludes the study.

3.2 Theoretical Framework

We defined the secondary sector of the Indian economy as an aggregation of activities including manufacturing, construction, electricity, gas and water supply. For the service sector we have employed a slightly modified taxonomy proposed by Fuchs[4] (1968) and include hotels, restaurants, wholesale and retail trade, banking, real estate, insurance, public administration, defence, transport, communication and other services. We now state the three hypotheses regarding the relative growth of employment in the service sector.

First, services have an income elasticity greater than one.[5] As a result, as real per capita income increases, real services per capita grow more than proportionately with income. Thus services account for an increasing share of national income and national employment.

Second, as economic specialisation and automation increase, the quality of service increases or their average cost falls, which in turn increases the demand[6] for and production of some service.

Third, the slower labour productivity[7] growth in this sector compared to that of the secondary sector explains the growing relative importance of the service sector in national employment.

The paper tests all the three hypotheses in the context of the Indian economy (1964–65 to 1984–85). The period has been restricted by the non-availability of adequate statistical data.

3.2.1 The model

This model is an extended version of Baumol's original two-sector model. There are two sectors — the Secondary Sector (*S*) comprising manufacturing, construction, electricity, gas and water supply and the Tertiary Sector (*T*) comprising hotel, trade, restaurants, public administration, defence, banking, real insurance and other services. The production technologies are represented by

$$Q_s = a \cdot L_s \cdot e^{(ls)\,t} \tag{3.1}$$

and

$$Q_t = b \cdot L_T \cdot e^{\,(l_T)\,t} \tag{3.2}$$

where output levels in time 't' (t subscripts are omitted), Q_s and Q_T depend upon the labour inputs, L_s and L_T and the rate of increase in labour productivity l_s and l_T. The total labour force is $L_s + L_T = L$.

The demand for the two outputs is described by the budget constraint (equal to the wage per worker, W), and the demand for one of the outputs, in this case services, is:

$$Q_{T/L} = C.(P_T/P_s)^\beta . W^\alpha . e^{r.t} \tag{3.3}$$

and

$$P_s .(Q_s/L) = W - P_T (Q_T/L) \tag{3.4}$$

Equation (3.3) is the demand for service per worker, which depends upon the relative price of services to the secondary sector (P_T/P_s), wage income per worker (W) and an exogenous shift in demands at the rate γ over time. The co-efficient β is the price-elasticity and α is the income-elasticity of demand for services. Equation (3.4) defines the demand for the secondary sector's output as the difference between wage income and expenditure on services. We can assume the secondary sector's output to be the numeraire; so that, $P_s \equiv 1$.

In the labour market, wages are determined in competitive conditions by equating the demand for labour to the supply of labour (L). A profit-maximizing firm will employ labour until the value of the marginal product of a unit of labour equals the wage. The marginal product of labour in the two sectors can be defined as:

$$\partial Q_s /\partial L_s = a \cdot e^{\,l_{s.t}} \tag{3.5}$$

$$\partial Q_T /\partial L_T = b \cdot e^{\,l_{T.t}} \tag{3.6}$$

Now equating the value of the marginal products of the secondary sector to the wage gives

$$W = P_s ae^{\,l_{s.t}} \tag{3.7}$$

Since,

$$P_s \equiv 1, \text{ then } W = a.e^{\,l_{s.t}} \tag{3.7a}$$

Market prices for the secondary sector's output and services are set in competitive markets, where the price must equal marginal cost.

With only one input, the marginal cost can be calculated by dividing the wage by marginal product. However, only the relative prices (P_T/P_s) are relevant for our analysis. They are defined as:

$$(P_T / P_s) = \left(\frac{a}{b}\right) \cdot e\, (l_s - l_T) \tag{3.8}$$

Using equations (3.5) and (3.6).

We can now describe the time path of the share of services in total employment in the simple economy. By definition, the share of services in total employment is:

$$\frac{L_T}{L_s + L_T} = \frac{L_T}{L} = \hat{L}_T. \tag{3.9}$$

From the production function for services (eqn. 3.2), we know :

$$L_T = \left(\frac{1}{b}\right) \cdot Q_T \cdot e^{-l_T \cdot t} \tag{3.10}$$

or in per-worker units

$$\frac{L_T}{L} = \left(\frac{1}{b}\right) \cdot \left(\frac{Q_T}{L}\right) \cdot e^{-l_T \cdot t} \tag{3.10a}$$

In equilibrium, the service output per worker (Q_T / L) must equal the service demand per worker given by equation (3.3) for the equilibrium relative prices (eqn. 3.8) and the equilibrium wage (eqn. 3.7):

$$QT / L = C\{(a/b) \cdot e^{(l\,s-l\,T)}\}^\beta \{a \cdot e^{Ls^t}\}\alpha \cdot e^{r.t} \tag{3.11}$$

$$\{(l_s - l_T)\beta + \alpha\, l_s + r\} \cdot t$$

or,

$$Q_T / L = A \cdot e \tag{3.11a}$$

where $A = (c / b^\beta) \cdot a^{\alpha+\beta}$. Substituting eqn. (3.11a) for (3.10a), the equilibrium path of service's share of total employment can be obtained:

$$L_T / L = \hat{L}_T = (A/b) \cdot e^{\{(l_s - l_T)\beta \cdot + \alpha\, l_s + \gamma - l_T\} \cdot t} \tag{3.12}$$

The rate of change of this share over time is

$$\frac{d(L_T / L)/d_t}{L_T / L} = \hat{\hat{L}}_T = (l_s - l_T)\beta + (l_s\,\alpha - l_T) + \gamma$$

or it can be arranged as $\hat{\hat{L}}_T = (\alpha - 1) \cdot l_s + \gamma + (l_s - l_T)(1 + \beta)$.

Thus, the rate of growth over time in the relative share of service employment is given by

$$\hat{\hat{L}}_T = (\alpha - 1) \cdot l_s + (l_s - l_T)(1 + \beta) + \gamma \qquad (3.13)$$

It is clear that this rate depends crucially on three factors, namely: the growth of labour-productivity of the secondary sector, the difference in the growth of labour-productivity in the two sectors and the rate of growth of the exogenous demand in the economy. There may be a number of other explanatory variables but we have restricted ourselves to the hypotheses we have proposed to test owing to the non-availability of statistical data, especially data relating to the prices of the different kinds of services. Before stating the results, we will discuss the definitions and the measurement techniques of the different variables.

It can be stated that a change in the specification of the demand equation as given in eqn. (3.3) can end up with an employment growth equation different from the one given by eqn. (3.13). If one replaces the wage W in eqn. (3.3) by a per capita income variable like Y/L, then it would be a consistent demand equation which can well be fitted to the model. But, replacement of W by Y/L will result in a Pi, which stands for the price of the i th services sector. In this exercise we will calculate the value of Pi where i stands for health, education, etc., sub-sectors of the service sector. This will be used to operationalize the regression analysis that follows.

3.3   Definitions and Measurement

The time series data used in the study are drawn primarily from the different volumes of *Indian Labour Statistics, Monthly Abstract of Statistics* and *Indian Database*. We have also relied heavily on the publications of the different Ministries of the Government of India. This includes the publications of the Ministry of Health and Family Welfare, Ministry of Human Resource Development, Ministry of Information and Broadcasting. We have also used data published by the Central Statistical Organization. A discussion of the principal concepts and sources follows.

3.3.1 Output

Output can be measured either by estimates of the Gross Domestic Product (GDP) or by Net Value Added (NVA) originating in each sector. To estimate real GDP and NVA, we have deflated the nominal values by the wholesale price index.[8]

GDP is not a fully satisfactory measure of real output but it is probably the best suited for productivity analysis. The most important defect of the GDP measure is that its components are, in some cases, estimated from employment data. This problem is most serious in government industries and some of the other industries in the service sector. Because of this problem we do not use GDP here. Hence we have taken real NVA as the index of output of the two sectors. NVA is more reliable since it is not derived out of employment data. The average annual growth rate has been calculated to fit a semi-log trend equation for the period 1964–68 to 1984–85.[9]

3.3.2 Employment

The "Number of Persons Engaged in Production," data which is available from the *Indian Labour Statistics* series, is used to measure employment. This series includes the self-employed as well as the employees reduced to full-time equivalents. However, the exclusion of unpaid family workers may introduce some measurement error in trade, while the method of converting part-time employment into full-time equivalents may introduce some bias in industries, such as services, where part-time employment is significant. The trend rate of growth has also been calculated fitting a semi-log trend equation.[10]

3.3.3 Total labour input

Employment data may not provide a completely satisfactory measure of total labour input for several reasons. First, there are possible defects in the employment series created by converting part-time employment to full-time equivalents. Second, there is the problem of obtaining accurate information concerning the average number of hours actually worked each year by full-time workers. Third, interpreting changes in man-hours would be problematic even if accurate data were available. In the unorganised service sector there are frequent cases where workers work substantially more than 48 hrs/week. In these cases, decrease in weekly hours, may be offset in part by an increase in effective labour input per hour due to reduced fatigue. Finally, the man-hours data tells us nothing about the quality of labour attributable to differences in intelligence, strength, training and so on. It would be useful to have a measure of labour input which takes into account all of these factors.

We may develop such a measure using the data on labour compensation.[11] Total labour compensation includes wages and salaries and the labour income of the self-employed. If we assume that the price of labour (adjusted for quality, effort, etc.) changes at the same rate in these two sectors of the economy, then the change in total labour compensation in a particular industry relative to change in the economy as a whole is equal to the change in labour input in that industry relative to the change in labour input for the economy as a whole.

The estimates of total labour compensation are based on the time series data available from the *Annual Survey of Industries and Indian Database*. The average annual rate of the growth trend of labour compensation has been estimated fitting a semi-log trend equation.

3.3.4   Productivity

Productivity is always shown as a residual of the difference between the rate of change of real output and the rate of change of whatever input or combination of inputs we are concerned with at the moment. Two of the variants of productivity[12] — the output per unit of labour input and the output per unit of total factor input—can be employed. In this study, we define productivity as the difference between the rate of change of real NVA and the rate of change of real labour compensation.

3.3.5   Different types of elasticities — price and income

The prices of different types of services play an important role in determining how attractive the services are relative to commodities for a nation. The rising prices can be expected to have a dampening effect on the purchase of services. Thus their ad hoc demand curve should have a negative slope whether or not they meet the formal conditions of demand theory. The measurement of price elasticities[13] for different types of services is very difficult simply because of the non-availability of statistical data on prices of different types of services. The equation estimated here is of the form

$$\log E_i = a + b \log Y + C \log P_i + Ui$$

where E_i is the real per capita expenditure on i th services, Y is the real per capita income and P_i is the price of i th services, C is the price elasticity and U_i is the standard disturbance term with zero mean and constant variance.

Since the price data of different types of services are not readily available we have calculated the price indices for the different types of services for different years by dividing the value index by quantity indices. For example, in the case of broadcasting services, we have first collected data on total expenditure on broadcasting (including mainly media like radio and TV) and then calculated the total number of people covered by the broadcasting system (which may be an index to quantity). Dividing the annual data of expenditure by the population in the respective year, we have got the prices for different years. In the case of educational services for governmental institutions, we have taken the costs of different types of education (viz., primary, middle, higher secondary and above) as proxy variables for price because in most of the cases governmental institutions are not profit making industries. In the case of family welfare, we have first calculated the total expenditure on family welfare, and then calculated the total number of married couples (which may be an approximation of the output of these services), and finally dividing the former by the latter, we got the prices for different years. In certain cases we have had to depend on the consumer price index of the urban non-manual employees (in case of all services and other governmental services).

As far as the income elasticity is concerned, there is no such problem as in the case of price elasticities. Here we have analysed the income elasticity separately for government and private services. The values thus obtained vary across the different types of services.[14] We have employed the value of the income elasticity for all services as the final and optimal value.

3.3.6 Results

The values of price elasticities for the different types of services vary from a low of −0.4 to a high of −0.9. The income elasticity of demand for all services is as high as 1.87; though income elasticities for the different types of domestic services provided by the government are just greater than 1. It assumes a value of 1.41 in the case of administration services provided by the government, while for broadcasting services it is 1.44.

The expenditure equation has been estimated by the method of Ordinary Least Square (OLS) and in almost all the cases the R square is high. The 't' values are significant and the D.W. statistics is close to 2. The details of the regression results obtained have not been reported for reasons of space.

We have already mentioned that labour productivity can be measured by taking the difference between the growth of real NVA and the growth of real labour compensation. We have reported only the values of labour productivities for our purpose. The value we have obtained for labour productivity in the secondary sector, is .0027 and for the tertiary sector is .0001. Next, we substitute the value of the income elasticity of demand for the tertiary sector's output as 1.87 and the price elasticity of demand for that sector as –0.9 in eqn. 3.13. We calculate the value of the rate of growth of exogenous demand as .0034, using the growth rate of employment of the tertiary sector eqn. (3.13).

So, $.0059 = (1.87–1) \times .0027 + (.0027– .0001)(1 – .9) + \gamma$

or, $.0059 = .0022 + .0003 + \gamma$

or, $\gamma = .0034$.

The above equation suggests that only 5 per cent employment growth (.0003/.0055 × 100) can be explained by the difference in labour productivity. The exogenous demand factor, as far as our result is concerned, can explain 57 per cent (.0034/ .0059 × 100) of the employment growth, and the growth of labour productivity in the secondary sector accounts for 37 per cent (.0022/ .0059 × 100) of the employment growth in the tertiary sector.

If we take the other extreme value of price elasticity of demand for the services output as –0.4, then we can claim that nearly 26 per cent of the explanation (.0075/.0055 × 100) of employment growth in the tertiary sector is accounted for by the differential labour productivity growth.[15] Here, again the exogenous demand factor accounts for 37 per cent (.0022/.0055 × 100) of total employment growth in the services sector while another 37 per cent is accounted for by relative labour productivity growth in the secondary sector.

3.4   Conclusions

At the outset, we proposed three hypotheses. Now it is time to consider these hypotheses in the light of the empirical findings that we have obtained for the Indian economy.

As far as our first hypothesis is concerned there is little doubt that services have an income elasticity greater than one. This means that as real per capita income increases, real services per capita grow more than proportionally. Thus services consume an increasing share of national income and national employment as well.

The second hypothesis can also be explained adequately with the empirical results we have obtained.

The crucial hypothesis of the slower relative growth of labour productivity in the service sector *vis-à-vis* the secondary sector cannot adequately explain the growing relative importance of the service sector in national employment in the light of the empirical results obtained here. So, the results for the Indian economy do not confirm Fuchs' (1968) and Baumol's (1967) hypotheses as formulated for the U.S. economy. The differential in the labour productivities in the secondary and in the tertiary sector cannot give us an adequate explanation for the relative growth of the services share in national employment *vis-à-vis* other sectors of the Indian economy.

One interesting finding we have obtained here relates to the role of demand for services in the national economy. We have seen earlier that the exogenous demand factor can give us an important explanation of the growth of employment in the service sector in our economy. Here again the traditional controversy between the 'supply constrained growth' and the 'demand limited growth' of the Indian economy has been revisited. So, finally, we can say that it is not the lagging labour productivity growth of the service sector *vis-à-vis* the secondary sector, but the rate of growth of exogenous demand for services which is mainly responsible for the relative growth of employment in the service sector of the Indian economy.

Notes

1. Baumol's original work can be found in 'Macroeconomics of Unbalanced Growth' in *American Economic Review*, 1967, 57: 415–26.
2. Fuchs (1985) has elaborated his view taking into consideration Baumol's model. Fuchs (1985) can be found in Inman (ed.), *Managing the Service Economy : Prospects and Problems*, Cambridge University Press, Cambridge, 1985.
3. Same as note 2.
4. Fuchs (1968) has defined the services sector in the book, *The Service Economy*, Ch. 2, Appendix I.
5. Fuchs (1968) has estimated an income elasticity of 1.50 for services generally, whereas Houthhakkar and Taylor (1966) have obtained

income elasticities for a wide variety of individual services in the range 0.5 to as high as 2.2. Most services have an income elasticity near 1.0.

6. Fuchs (1985) has concluded from a comparison of input-output tables for the years 1947 and 1958 of the U.S. economy that less than 10 per cent of the total growth in service employment can be attributed to the growth of intermediate demand by the goods producing industries.

7. Fuchs (1985) has concluded that faster technological change and improved labour quality in the industrial sector accounted for the majority of the productivity differences between industry and services during 1929 to 1965 in the U.S. economy.

   Haig (1975) tested Fuchs' three hypotheses for the relative growth of employment in the service sector in the Australian economy over the period 1960–1970. The conclusion is that lagging labour productivity growth in the service sector is a major determinant of the relative growth of employment in the service sector in the Australian economy.

8. Fuchs (1964) employed this type of definition in *Productivity Trends in Goods and Service Sectors – 1929–61, A Preliminary Survey* - Ch. 2, p. 7.

9. To find the trend value of variables, we have taken a semi-log trend equation of the form,

   $ln\ Y = a + bT$. Where, Y is the value of the variable, a is constant and 'T' is time trend, coefficient b is significant at two tails test at 5 per cent level of significance.

10. Same as 9 above.

11. The idea can be found in Fuchs (1964). For the formula one can see the Appendix, of the same volume.

12. For definition of labour productivity one can see Fuchs (1986), Ch.3, and Kendrick's (1985) paper in Inman (ed), *Managing the Service Economy, Prospects and Problems*, Cambridge University Press, Cambridge, 1985.

13. Price elasticity estimates for the government services range from –.2 to –.8 [Inman (1978b)] and for private services from –.4 to –1.6 [Houthhakkar and Taylor (1966)].

14. See note 5 above.

15. If we employ Kendrick's (1985) definition of labour productivity growth, then the result will be different.

References

Baumol, W.J. (1967). Macroeconomics of Unbalanced Growth. *American Economic Review* June, 57: 415–26.

Chandhok, H.L. and the Policy Group. (1990). *Indian Database: The Economy, Annual Time Series Data*, Vol. I and II. Faridabad, Haryana: Thompson Press.

Fuchs, V.R. (1968). *The Service Economy*. New York: National Bureau of Economic Research, General Series, No. 87.

(1964). *Productivity Trends in the Goods and Service Sectors, 1929–61: A Preliminary Survey*. New York: National Bureau of Economic Research, O.P.89.

(1965), *Importance of Service and Industries*. New York: National Bureau of Economic Research, O.P.96.

Fuchs, V.R. and J.A. Wilburn. (1967). *Productivity Difference within the Services Sector*. New York: National Bureau of Economic Research, O.P.102.

Government of India. *Economic Survey* (various issues). Ministry of Finance.

Indian Labour Statistics (various issues). Simla: Government of India Press, Labour Bureau, Ministry of Labour.

Indian Labour Year Book (various issues). Simla: Government of India Press, Labour Bureau, Ministry of Labour.

Monthly Abstract of Statistics (various issues). New Delhi: Central Statistical Organisation, Department of Statistics, Ministry of Planning and Programme Implementation.

Haig, B.D. (1975). An Analysis of Change in the Distribution of Employment between Manufacturing and Service Industries, 1960–1970. *The Review of Economics and Statistics* 57: 35–42.

Houthhakkar and Taylor (1966). *Consumer Demand in the United States, 1929–1970*. Cambridge, Mass.: Harvard University Press.

Inman (ed.) (1985). *Managing the Service Economy : Prospects and Problems*. Cambridge, U.K.: Cambridge University Press.

(1978b). The Fiscal Performance of Local Governments : An Interpretative Review. In P. Mieszkowski and M. Straszheim (eds), *Current Issues in Urban Economics*, 270–321. Baltimore: The Johns Hopkins University Press.

Kendrick, J.W. (1956). *Productivity Trends: Capital and Labour*. New York: National Bureau of Economic Research, O.P.53.

(1961). *Productivity Trends in the United States*. Princeton: Princeton University Press.

(1985). Measurement of Output and Productivity in the Service Sector. In Inman (ed), *Managing the Service Economy : Prospects and Problems*. Cambridge, U.K.: Cambridge University Press.

Kravis, I.B., A. Heston and R. Summers. (1982). *World Product and Income — International Comparison of Real Gross Product*. Baltimore: The Johns Hopkins University Press.

Stiglar, G.J. (1956). *Trends in Employment in Service Industry*. Princeton: Princeton University Press, National Bureau of Economic Research.

Food Levy and the Public Distribution System: A Two-Sector Analysis

Kaushik Gupta

4.1 Introduction

The purpose of this paper is to examine the economic implications of the effects of levy on food under a two-sector framework in a developing economy like India. The literature on food policies and the public distribution of foodgrains is quite extensive. One can refer to the works of Patnaik (1975), Kahlon and Tyagi (1983), George (1984), Bose (1985), Das (1987) and Dasgupta (1988). The motivation for this study originates from the fact that the study of effects of food levy on producers in a developing economy is neglected in the literature. The present study attempts to fill this lacuna in theoretical literature.

The analysis is carried out in a Rakshit–Taylor framework[1] [Rakshit 1982; Taylor 1983] which relates to the dualism between agriculture and industry in a developing economy like India. We assume that the economy is divided into two sectors — agriculture and industry. The assumptions regarding the two sectors are similar to those of the standard Rakshit–Taylor type two-sector models. Further, the agricultural sector produces food whereas the industrial sector produces a good which is used for both consumption and investment purposes. There exist three classes in society — the capitalists, the farmers and the industrial workers. The industrial good is consumed by all the three classes, whereas food is consumed by the industrial workers alone. Consumption of food by the farmers is considered only in the context of the microfoundation of the marketed surplus function and is netted out from the rest of the two-sector analysis. It is assumed that the industrial workers do not save and that they spend a fraction of their nominal income on food and the remaining part of their income on the industrial good.

The main conclusion of this paper is the following: In a developing economy the government's inclination to increase the amount or the price of levy is not always desirable. It may create inflationary pressures within the economy by raising the open-market price and reducing the level of industrial output except under certain assumptions. This paper also points out that under this framework of levy even if the ration price is reduced, the open-market price will increase.

For the sake of simplicity the levy which we consider here is a levy on the producers which is a fixed or lump-sum part of the total marketed surplus of food. The two-sector model with fixed levy on food is considered in Section 4.2. In Section 4.3. we consider some food policy measures in the context of our two-sector analysis. Section 4.4. summarises the main results of the paper.

4.2 The Model with Fixed Levy on Food

4.2.1 The agricultural sector

The agricultural sector produces a single commodity which we shall refer to as 'food'. The marketed surplus of food (X) is an increasing function of the open-market price (P_X). The other arguments are the levy price (P_l) and the quantity of levy ($\overline{X}_l$). Thus, we have

$$X = (P_X, P_l, \overline{X}_l) \tag{4.1}$$

$$X_1 > 0, \quad X_2 < 0 \text{ and } X_3 \gtreqless 0 \text{ accordingly as } P_X \gtreqless P_l$$

In eqn. (4.1) X_i (for $i = 1,2,3$) implies the impact of each of the arguments i.e. P_X, P_l and $\overline{X}_l$ on X. The farmers sell the marketed surplus X both to the government (in the form of levy) at the levy price (P_l) and to the open-market at the open-market price (P_X). In order to justify the form of the marketed surplus function we need to establish the microfoundation of eqn. (4.1) which is shown in Appendix 1. We consider here only the intuitive reasoning.

An increase in P_X raises the total supply of food by the farmers and reduces their home consumption of food (if we assume that the farmers purchase food produced by them at the open-market price). The net result is an increase in the marketed surplus as a result of an increase in P_X. An increase in P_l raises the income of the farmers. Since the income effect on food consumption by the farmers is positive, given the total supply of food, the marketed surplus will be reduced. The question of whether an increase in the quantity of levy increases the income of the farmer or not, can be answered by comparing the open-market price and the levy price. If $P_X > P_l$, an increase in $\overline{X}_l$ reduces the amount supplied to the open-market and hence reduces the income of the farmers, whereas if, $P_x < P_l$, by the same logic an increase in $\overline{X}_l$ increases the income of the farmers. Thus, given the supply of food, the effect on home consumption of food and the effect on marketed surplus of food due to an increase or decrease in income of the farmers resulting from an increase in $\overline{X}_l$ depends on the values of P_X and P_l. Generally, $X_3 \gtreqless 0$ accordingly as $P_X \gtreqless P_l$.

As stated earlier, consumption of food by the farmers is netted out from our two-sector analysis. It is required only to establish eqn. 4.1. Thus, in our two-sector analysis, the industrial workers are the only consumers of food. The industrial workers' demand for food (X^d) is given by the following specification:

$$X^d = X^d (P_X, w\,\theta Y, P_r, \overline{X}_r) \tag{4.2}$$

where $X_1^d < 0, X_2^d > 0, X_3^d < 0, X_4^d > 0$ and

$$\left| \frac{X_1^d \, P_X}{X^d} \right| < 1$$

In eqn. (4.2) X_i^d (for $i = 1, 2, 3, 4$) the impact of each of the arguments, i.e., P_x, w, θY, P_r and $\bar{X}_r$, on X^d, w implies the wage rate of the industrial workers, θ is the fixed labour-output coefficient ratio and Y is industrial output such that $W\theta Y$ is the worker's income; P_r is the ration price of food and $\bar{X}_r$ is the amount supplied through ration shops. If we assume that food is a non-inferior good to the industrial workers then an increase in Y causes an upward shift of the demand curve such that X_2^d is positive. The signs of other partial derivatives can be explained as follows:

The inverse relation between X^d and P_X follows from any standard demand function for normal goods (i.e. $X_1^d < 0$). A decrease in P_r increases the demand for food since it increases the purchasing power of the workers. The workers can purchase the same basket of food by spending less, which is equivalent to an increase in income.[2] The change in income resulting from a change in P_r is given as $|\bar{X}_r\, dP_r|$ and in real terms as $|\bar{X}_r/P_X\, dP_r|$. Let α be the fraction which the workers spend on food and the remaining part of it on the industrial good. Thus,

$$X_3^d = -\frac{\alpha \bar{X}_r}{P_X} < 0 \qquad\qquad (4.3)$$

The negative sign implies that due to a fall in P_r, the income effect increases the demand for X. Similarly, an increase in $\bar{X}_r$ increases the availability of food at the subsidized price.

The workers can either purchase more food or at least purchase the same basket of food at a lower cost. The reduction in the workers' expenditure, which is equivalent to an increase in their income, is given by[3] $(P_X - P_r)\, d\bar{X}_r$. Thus, in real terms the increase in income of the workers is given as $(P_X - P_r/P_X)\, d\bar{X}_r$. Thus,

$$X_4^d = \frac{\alpha\,(P_X - P_r)}{P_X} > 0 \qquad\qquad (4.4)$$

Our next assumption is regarding the nature of levy. Here we consider levy as a particular form of procurement. For the sake of simplicity we assume that the amount levied by the government is to be distributed to the consumers at a subsidized price called the ration or issue price. In other words, the levy is sufficient to meet the subsistence consumption needs of the workers provided by the ration shops, but is insufficient to maintain the economy's buffer stock. Thus,

$$\bar{X}_l = \bar{X}_r \qquad\qquad (4.5)$$

As the industrial workers are the only consumers of food[4] in this two-sector analysis, the marketed surplus of food provided by the farmers is equal to the total demand for food by the industrial workers in equilibrium, i.e.,

$$X(P_X, P_l, \overline{X}_l) = X^d(P_X, w\theta Y, P_r, \overline{X}_r) \qquad (4.6)$$

The Rakshit–Taylor type assumptions ensure that the open-market price adjusts to clear the food market. As a result, it is sufficient to consider the equilibrium condition for the open market food rather than for the agricultural sector as a whole. The marketed surplus of food for the open market only is given as $[X(P_X, P_l, \overline{X}_l) - \overline{X}_l]$. The open-market demand for food is given as $[X^d(P_X, w\theta Y, P_r, \overline{X}_r) - \overline{X}_r]$. Thus, the equilibrium condition in the open-market food is

$$X(P_X, P_l, \overline{X}_r) - \overline{X}_l = X^d(P_X, w\theta Y, P_r, \overline{X}_r) - \overline{X}_r \qquad (4.7)$$

Due to eqn. (4.5) one can observe that (4.8) and (4.7) are equivalent.

The locus of all combinations of Y and P_X that equilibrate the food market — as given by eqn. (4.6) or (4.7) — is called the XX curve (see Figure 4.1), the slope of which is positive and is stated as

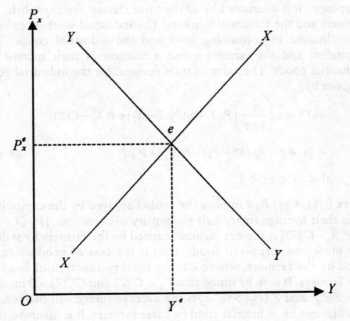

Fig. 4.1

$$\frac{dP_X}{dY}\bigg|_{XX} = \frac{w\theta X_2^d}{X_1 - X_1^d} > 0 \tag{4.8}$$

Thus, if we start from any combination (Y, P_X) at which the food market is in equilibrium, we find that an increase in P_X will lead to an increase in the open-market supply of food and a decrease in the open-market demand for the same. Hence Y must increase to maintain the balance in the open-market for food.

4.2.2 The Industrial Sector

Following the usual Rakshit–Taylor type assumptions we consider that the industrial sector is characterized by excess capacity and its output is demand-determined. The price of the industrial product (P_Y) is fixed on a mark-up basis and can be stated as

$$P_Y = (1+\gamma)\, w.\, \theta \tag{4.9}$$

where γ measures the mark-up or the degree of monopoly. Here we consider w and P_Y to be fixed.

The industrial good is used for consumption and investment purposes. It is consumed by all the three classes: the capitalists, the farmers and the industrial workers. The industrial workers exhaust their income in consuming food and the industrial goods. The capitalists and the farmers spend a fraction of their income on industrial goods. The value of total demand for the industrial good is given by

$$P_Y Y^d = c_1\left(\frac{\gamma}{1+\gamma}\right) P_Y\, Y + c_2[P_X\, X - \overline{X}_l) + P_l\, \overline{X}_l - C(Z)]$$

$$+ \; [w\cdot\theta\, Y - P_X\,(X^d - \overline{X}_r) - P_r\, \overline{X}_r] + P_Y\, \overline{I} \tag{4.10}$$

$$0 < c_1 < c_2 < 1$$

Here $(\gamma/(1+\gamma))\, P_Y\, Y$ implies the profits enjoyed by the capitalists. c_1 is their average (marginal) propensity to consume. $[P_X\,(X - \overline{X}_l) + P_l\overline{X}_l - C\,(Z)]$ is the net income[5] earned by the farmers by selling the marketed surplus of food. $C(Z)$ is the cost of production of food by the farmers, where Z is the total production of food by the farmers. It is to be noted that $P_X = C'(Z)$ and $C''(Z) > 0$ implies $Z = Z(P_X)$ and $Z'(P_X) > 0$. c_2 is the average (marginal) propensity to consume an industrial good by these farmers. It is assumed that $c_2 > c_1$. $[w\theta Y - P_X\,(X^d - \overline{X}_r) - P_r\, \overline{X}_r]$ is the expenditure of the industrial workers on industrial products and $\bar{I}$ is the amount of autonomous investment in real terms.

Considering the assumption that the output in the industrial sector is demand-determined, we can write

$$P_Y Y = c_1 \left(\frac{\gamma}{1+\gamma} \right) P_Y \cdot Y + c_2 [P_X (X - \bar{X}_l) + P_l \bar{X}_l - C(Z)]$$

$$+ \left[w \, \theta t Y - P_X (X^d - \bar{X}_r) - P_r \bar{X}_r \right] + P_Y \bar{I} \tag{4.11}$$

The locus of all combinations of Y and P_X that equilibrate the market for the industrial good — as given by equation (4.11) — is called the YY curve (see Figure 4.1), the slope of which is negative in the neighbourhood of equilibrium and is stated as

$$\left. \frac{dP_X}{dY} \right|_{YY} = \frac{\left(\dfrac{\gamma}{1+\gamma} \right) P_Y (1 - c_1) + P_X w \cdot \theta \, X_2^d}{(c_2 \, G_{P_X} - L_{P_X}) - c_2 C'(Z) Z'} < 0 \tag{4.12}$$

$$G_{P_X} = (X - \bar{X}_l) + P_X X_l$$

$$L_{P_X} = (X^d - \bar{X}_r) + P_X X_1^d$$

where G_{P_X} is the increase in the value of marketed surplus as P_X rises by one unit and L_{P_X} is the additional expenditure on food by the industrial workers as P_X rises by one unit in the neighbourhood of equilibrium $G_{P_X} = L_{P_X}$.

The combination (Y^e, P_X^e) in Figure 4.1 denotes the point of simultaneous equilibrium in both the food market and the market for industrial goods. The fact that the XX curve is positively sloped and the YY curve is negatively sloped implies that the equilibrium is stable. (For proof see Appendix 2).

The economic interpretation of the slope of YY is as follows. An increase in P_X by one unit leads to an increase in the expenditure on food by the industrial workers by L_{P_X} as $|X_1^d P / X^d| < 1$. L_{P_X} is equal to the decline in expenditure on industrial goods by the industrial workers as P_X rises by one unit. In the neighbourhood of equilibrium, L_{P_X} is also equal to the additional income accruing to the farmers by selling the marketed surplus as a result of an increase in P_X, i.e. G_{P_X}. Again an increase in P_X raises food supply (Z) and hence the cost of food production $C(Z)$. Hence the increase in net income of the farmers as a result of an increase in P_X, i.e. $c_2 [G_{P_X} - C'(Z) Z']$, is less than L_{P_X} (i.e. the decline in the industrial workers' expenditure on the industrial good). Thus the total demand for the industrial good, and hence Y, declines ultimately. If $G_{P_X} < C'(Z) Z'$ there is a decrease in the net income of the farmers and in that case the total demand for the industrial good (and consequently Y) will definitely decline as a result of an increase in P_X. Thus, the YY curve is negatively sloped in the neighbourhood of equilibrium.

4.3 Alternative Food Policies: Some Comparative Static Exercises

As the equilibrium shown by the intersection of the XX and the YY curves in Figure 4.1 is stable, we can pass on to our comparative static exercises one by one. These are actually the various food policy measures which are used by the government in a developing economy like India.[6]

4.3.1 Simultaneous increase in the quantity of levy $(\overline{X}_l)$ and the amount supplied through the ration shops $(\overline{X}_r)$.

An increase in the quantity of levy $(\overline{X}_l)$ matched by an increase in the amount supplied through ration shops $(\overline{X}_r)$ will lead to an increase or decrease in marketed surplus of food by $X^d_3 d\overline{X}_l$ on the one hand and to an increase in the demand for food by the industrial workers by the amount $X_4^d d\overline{X}_r$ on the other. In less developed countries we generally find[7] $P_X > P_l$ so that $X_3 > 0$. Thus, an increase in $\overline{X}_l = \overline{X}_r$ will lead to an increase in both the marketed surplus and the demand for food by the industrial workers. Both these effects operate through the income effect — the increase in $\overline{X}_l$ operates through the income-effect on home consumption of food by the farmers whereas, $\overline{X}_r$ operates through the income effect on food consumption by the industrial workers. If we assume that the income-effect related to the home consumption of food by the farmers is high such that $X_3 > X_4^d$ we get an excess supply in the food market. As a result of this, given Y at Y^e (the initial equilibrium level), P_X will fall to clear the market. Again the market is cleared if, given P_X at P_x^e, Y is gradually increased so that the demand curve shifts to the right until excess supply falls to zero and a new equilibrium is reached. In this case the XX curve will shift downward to the right.

In the industrial sector, given Y and P_X, increase in $\overline{X}_l$ leads to an increase in the demand for the industrial product by the farmers by the amount $|c_2 P_X X_3\, d\overline{X}_l\,|$ and a decrease in demand for the same by the farmers by the amount $|C_2 (P_1 - P_X)\, d\overline{X}_l\,|$ under the assumption $P_x > P_l$. An equivalent increase in $\overline{X}_r$ implies an increase in the purchasing power of the industrial workers and consequently an increase in their demand for the industrial product by the amount $(1 - \alpha)\,(P_X - P_r)\, d\overline{X}_l$. Thus, the total change in demand for the industrial product is

$$[c_2 (P_l - P_X) + c_2 P_X X_3 + (1 - \alpha)(P_X - P_r)]\, d\overline{X}_l =$$
$$[c_2 (P_l - P_r) + (P_X - P_r)(1 - \alpha - c_2) + c_2 P_X X_3]\, d\overline{X}_l.$$

As in less developed countries P_r is low enough to provide the subsistence requirements of consumers at a low cost, we can assume[8] $P_l > P_r$. Thus, the change in the demand for $_Y$ is positive if $(1 - \alpha) > c_2$. Hence, when $P_X > P_l > P_r$ and $(1 - \alpha) > c_2$,[9] given P_X at P_X^e, the industrial output will increase as it is demand-determined. In other words, the YY curve will shift to the right.[10]

Thus, when both the XX and the YY curves shift to the right to $X_1 X_1$ and $Y_1 Y_1$ the industrial output will increase. However, the effect on the open market price is ambiguous. For a graphical depiction we can

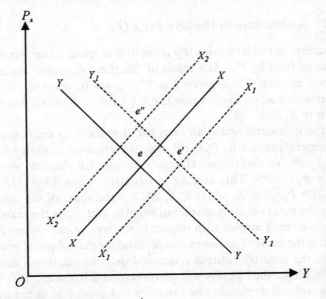

Fig. 4.2 Increase in $\overline{X}_l = \overline{X}_r$

consider Figure 4.2. The initial equilibrium is at e whereas the final equilibrium is at e'.

Suppose in the food market we consider $X_3 < X^d_4$ (X_3 being positive as $P_X > P_l$), i.e., a situation of excess demand in the food market when Y and P_X are at the initial equilibrium level, then given Y at Y^e, P_X will increase to clear the market. In this situation the XX curve will shift upwards to the left to $X_2 X_2$.[11] Here the effect on the industrial sector will be similar to that in the earlier situation, i.e., YY will shift to the right to $Y_1 Y_1$. The new equilibrium (point e'' in Figure 4.2) is characterized by a higher open market price. However, the effect on the industrial output in this situation is ambiguous.

We now summarise our results in the form of a proposition (For mathematical treatment of this analysis see Appendix 3).

Proposition 1: Under the following assumptions: (i) $P_X > P_l > P_r$, (ii) $(1 - \alpha) c_2$ and (iii) if the income effect related to the home consumption of food by the farmers is much stronger compared to the income-effect related to food consumption by industrial workers so that $X_3 > X^d_4$ we find that Y will increase whereas the effect on P_X is indeterminate as a result of an increase in $\overline{X}_l = \overline{X}_r$. The conclusions are opposite when assumption (iii) is changed to $X_3 < X^d_4$.

4.3.2   An increase in the levy price (P_l)

An increase in the levy price (P_l) leads to a decrease in the marketed surplus of food by X_2. As a result of this there is excess demand in the food market. Thus, given Y at Y^e, P_X will increase to clear the market which again implies that the XX curve will shift upwards to the left to $X_1 X_1$.[12]

In the industrial sector an increase in P_l leads to an increase in the farmers' income by $P_2 X_2 dP_l$ and to a decrease in their income by $P_2 X_2 dP_l$, so that the net change in income (in absolute terms) is $|(\overline{X}_l + P_2 X_2) dP_l|$. This change is negative when $|X_2 P_X|/\overline{X}_2 > 1$ or $|\varepsilon_{P_l}| > P_l \overline{X}_l / P_X X$, where $P_l \overline{X}_l / P_X X$ is the share of the value of levy in the total value of marketed surplus and ε_{P_l} is the elasticity of the marketed surplus with respect to the levy price.[13] When there is a fall in the farmers' incomes, the demand for the industrial product falls. As the industrial output is demand-determined, it will also fall, given P_X. Hence the YY curve will shift downwards to the left to $Y_1 Y_1$.[14] For a graphical depiction one can refer to Figure 4.3. In the figure the initial equilibrium is at e and corresponding to this the final

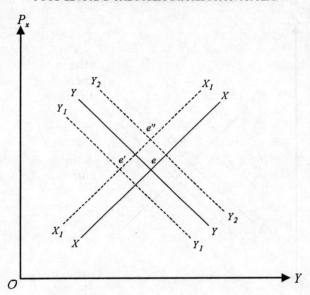

Fig. 4.3 Increase in P_l

equilibrium is at e'. It implies that an increase in P_l leads to a reduction in Y. However, the effect on P_X is ambiguous.

If, however, $|X_2 P_X / \overline{X}_l| < 1$ or $|\varepsilon_{P_l}| < P_l \overline{X}_l / P_X X$ the change in the farmers' income will be positive as a result of an increase in P_l. In this case, the demand for the industrial product and hence Y will increase, given P_X. Here the YY curve shifts upwards to the right[15] i.e., to $Y_2 Y_2$ as shown in Figure 4.3 and the new equilibrium is at e''. The new equilibrium is characterised by a higher open-market price with ambiguous changes in the industrial output.

We summarise our results in the form of the following proposition by comparing the relative shifts of the XX and the YY curves (For mathematical details one can refer to Appendix 3).

Proposition 2: If $|\varepsilon_{P_l}| > P_l \overline{X}_l / P_X X$, we find that Y falls and P_X changes indeterminately as a result of an increase in P_l. If, however, $|\varepsilon_{P_l}| < P_l \overline{X}_l / P_X X$, the effect on Y is indeterminate, whereas P_X increases as a result of an increase in P_l.

4.3.3 A reduction in the ration price of food (P_r)

A decrease in the ration price of food leads to an increase in the demand for food by the industrial workers. As a result of this

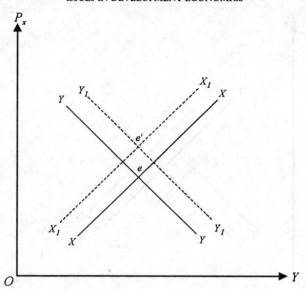

Fig. 4.4   Reduction in P_r

there is excess demand in the food market. Thus, given Y at Y^e, P_X will increase to clear the market, which again implies that the XX curve will shift upwards to the left to $X_1 X_1$.[16] This is shown in Figure 4.4.

Again, a reduction in P_r leads to an increase in the worker's demand for the industrial product by $|(1 - \alpha)\overline{X}_r \, dP_r|$, as a result of which the industrial output (Y) increases, given P_X at P^e_X. Thus, given $P_X = P^e_X$, the YY curve shifts to the right to $Y_1 Y_1$[17] so that the new equilibrium is at e', as shown in Figure 4.4. Our net result is summarized by comparing the relative shifts of the XX and the YY curves in the form of the following proposition. (For mathematical details one can refer to Appendix 3).

Proposition 3:   A reduction in the ration price of food (P_r) increases the open-market price of food. The effect on the industrial output, however, is ambiguous.

4.4   Conclusion

The major conclusion of this study is that in a developing economy the policies related to levy on food and the public distribution of foodgrains, except under some special circumstances, create inflationary pressures within the economy when industrial activity is constrained by the level of effective demand. It may also reduce industrial output together with this inflationary pressure. Whether the policy of voluntary procurement is more desirable compared to a levy is a different issue. Our purpose here is to chalk out a framework for a public distribution system which allows for a scheme of levy on the producers of food when the government finds it difficult to mobilize voluntary procurement of foodgrains.

Our study suggests that the policy of food levy is not desirable from two standpoints. First, except under certain special circumstances, policies related to levy on food raises the open market price. In some situations, we have the possibility that together with an increase in the open market price of food there is also a reduction in industrial output. It appears as if the industrial output increases under certain assumptions, when the food policy has to match an increase in the quantity of levy by an equivalent increase in the quantity supplied through ration shops. It also appears that the industrial output decreases when the levy price increases and that the elasticity of the marketed surplus with respect to the levy price is greater than the share of levy in the total marketed surplus in value terms. In these two situations the effect on the open-market price is uncertain thus dampening the incentive of the producers and leaving in question the open market purchase plan of the consumers.

Appendix 1

Microfoundation of the marketed surplus function

In order to establish the microfoundation of equation (4.1) we start with a representative farmer. We also assume that his behaviour is reflected at the aggregative level as shown in the text.

Let z be the total production of food and h be the consumption of food by a representative farmer. Then his marketed surplus of food (X) is given by:

$$x = z - h \tag{1}$$

The intuition behind eqn. (1) is the definition of marketed surplus, which is the total agricultural production minus home consumption of the agricultural product by the representative farmer. We formalize this home consumption by assuming that the farmer purchases food at the open-market price (P_X). Thus, the farmer is both the producer as well as the consumer of food.

The income (m) of the farmer is

$$m = P_X(z - \overline{X}_l) + P_l \overline{X}_l - c(z) \tag{2}$$

where P_l is the levy price and $\overline{X}_l$ is the quantity of levy imposed by the government on the farmer, $c(z)$ is the cost function with a rising marginal cost curve.

The farmer consumes food as well as the industrial product. Hence, his utility function is

$$u = u(h, n) \tag{3}$$

Where n is the consumption of the industrial product (Y) by the farmer. The utility function satisfies all the standard properties. The budget equation is

$$P_X h + P_Y n = m \tag{4}$$

The problem of the farmer is to maximize $u(h, n)$ subject to

$$P_X h + P_Y n = m$$

and

$$m = P_X(z - \overline{X}_l) + P_l \overline{X}_l - c(z)$$

with respect to h, n and z. For the sake of simplicity, this can be broken into two stages.

The *first stage* deals with maximization of income (m) with respect to production (z).

The first-order condition is

$$P_X = c'(z) \tag{5}$$

The price – marginal cost equality is the competitive equilibrium condition. As $c''(z) > 0$, we get

$$z = z(P_X) \tag{6}$$

where $z'(P_X) > 0$.

Relation (6) is the standard supply function, but this is not the marketed surplus function.

The *second stage* deals with the maximization of utility subject to maximum income. Suppose that m^* is the maximum income with respect to production z. Then,

$$m^* = P_X(z(P_X) - \overline{X}_l) + P_l \overline{X}_l - c(z(P_X)) \tag{7}$$

The problem of the farmer is to maximize $u\,(h, n)$ subject to $P_X h + P_Y n = m^*$.

If h and n are normal goods we get the demand function of the farmer for food as

$$h = h\,(P_X, m^*, P_Y) \tag{8}$$

where $h_1 < 0$ and $h_2 > 0$.

So the demand curve slopes negatively and shifts upwards when income rises. Thus,

$$\frac{\partial X}{\partial P_X} = \frac{\partial z\,(P_X)}{\partial P_X} - \frac{\partial h\,(P_X, m^*, P_Y)}{\partial P_X}$$

$$= [z' - h_1] > 0 \tag{9}$$

m^* is a function of P_1 [see relation (4.7)]

Thus, $\quad \dfrac{\partial m^*}{\partial P_l} = \overline{X}_l > 0 \tag{10}$

Hence, $\dfrac{\partial h}{\partial P_l} = \dfrac{\partial h}{\partial m^*}\dfrac{\partial m^*}{\partial P_l} > 0 \tag{11}$

This is because an increase in P_l raises the income, and the income effect on food is positive. From eqn. (1) we get,

$$\frac{\partial X}{\partial P_l} = - \frac{\partial h}{\partial P_l} < 0 \tag{12}$$

So the marketed surplus should be a negative function of the levy price. Similarly, an increase in the quantity of $\overline{X}_l$ reduces the farmers' income if $P_X > P_l$ and increases income if $P_l > P_X$. Thus, we have

$$\frac{\partial m^*}{\partial \overline{X}_l} = -(P_X - P_l) \lesseqgtr 0 \,,\ \text{accordingly as } P_X \gtreqless P_l \tag{13}$$

and $\dfrac{\partial h}{\partial \overline{X}_l} = \dfrac{\partial h}{\partial m^*}\dfrac{\partial m^*}{\partial \overline{X}_l} \lesseqgtr 0$ accordingly as $P_X \gtreqless P_l \tag{14}$

From (1) we get,

$$\frac{\partial X}{\partial \overline{X}_l} = - \frac{\partial h}{\partial \overline{X}_l} \gtreqless 0 \ \text{accordingly as } P_X \gtreqless P_l \tag{15}$$

Thus, the impact of $\overline{X}_l$ on x depends on whether $P_X \gtreqless P_l$.

Appendix 2

Stability of the system

The adjustment equations of the system are

$$\frac{dY}{dt} = F(Y^d - Y), \, F(0) = 0, \, F' > 0 \tag{16}$$

$$\frac{dP_X}{dt} = \psi(X^d - X), \, \psi(0) = 0, \, \psi' > 0 \tag{17}$$

The necessary and sufficient conditions for stability are:

$$-F'\left[(1-c_1)\left(\frac{\Gamma}{1+\Gamma}\right) + \frac{P_X w \, \theta \, X_2^d}{P_Y}\right] + \psi'\left(X_1^d - X_1\right)$$

$$= t_r \, J_E < 0 \tag{18}$$

$$\left\{-F'\left[(1-c_1)\left(\frac{\Gamma}{1+\Gamma}\right) + \frac{P_X w \, \theta \, X_2^d}{P_Y}\right]\right\}\left\{\psi'\left(X_1^d - X_1\right) - \right.$$

$$\left.\left\{\frac{F'}{P_Y}\left[(c_2 G_{P_X} - L_{P_X}) \, c_2 \, C'(Z)Z'\right]\right\}\left\{\psi' w \, \theta \, X_2^d\right\} = |J_E| > 0 \tag{19}$$

where J_E is the Jacobian evaluated at the equilibrium.
Here, the trace condition (as shown by eqn. (18)) is satisfied. The determinant condition eqn. (19), actually boils down to

$$\left.\frac{dY}{dP_X}\right|_{XX} - \left.\frac{dY}{dP_X}\right|_{YY} > 0$$

In the present model since $\left.\dfrac{dY}{dP_X}\right|_{XX} > 0$ and $\left.\dfrac{dY}{dP_X}\right|_{YY} < 0$, the condition is satisfied.

Appendix 3

Comparative static exercises

3.1   Increase in $\overline{X}_l = \overline{X}_r$

Differentiating eqn. (4.6) and (4.11) of the text with respect to $\overline{X}_l \, (= \overline{X}_r)$, we get

$$A_{11} \frac{dY}{d\bar{X}_l} + A_{12} \frac{dP_X}{d\bar{X}_l} = -(X_e - X_4^d) \tag{20}$$

$$A_{21} \frac{dY}{d\bar{X}_l} + A_{22} \frac{dP_X}{d\bar{X}_l} = c_2(P_l - P_X) + (P_X - P_r) + c_2 P_X X_3$$

$$- P_X X_4^d \tag{21}$$

Where $A_{11} = -w\theta X_2^d < 0$

$$A_{12} = (X_1 - X_1^d) > 0$$

$$A_{21} = \left[\left(\frac{\tau}{1+\tau}\right)P_Y(1-c_1) + P_X w\theta X_2^d\right] > 0$$

$$A_{22} = \left[c_2 G_{P_X} - L_{P_X} - c_2 C'(Z)Z'\right] > 0$$

The right-hand side of eqn. (21) can be simplified as follows using relation (4.4) of the text

$$c_2(P_1 - P_X) + (P_X - P_r) + c_2 P_X X_3 - P_X X_4^d$$

$$= c_2(P_l - P_r) + (P_X - P_r)[(1-\alpha) - c_2] + c_2 P_X X_3$$

If $P_X > P_l$, $X_3 > X_4^d$ and $(1 - \alpha) > c_2$, using Cramer's Rule, we can check $dY/d\bar{X}_l > 0$, whereas the sign of $dP_X/d\bar{X}_l$ is indeterminate. Again, when $X_3 < X_4^d$ we find $dY/d\bar{X}_l$ is indeterminate but $dP_X/d\bar{X}_l > 0$.

3.2 Increase in P_l

Differentiating eqn. (4.6) and (4.11) of the text with respect to P_l, we get

$$A_{11} \frac{dY}{dP_l} + A_{12} \frac{dP_X}{dP_l} = -X_2 \tag{22}$$

$$A_{21} \frac{dY}{dP_l} + A_{22} \frac{dP_X}{dP_l} = c_2(\bar{X}_l + P_X X_2) \tag{23}$$

The signs of $A_{ij}s$ (for $i = 1, 2; j = 1, 2$) are already mentioned above. The right hand side of equation (23) can be written as

$$c_2(\bar{X}_l + P_X X_2) = c_2 \bar{X}_l \left(1 + \frac{P_X X_2}{\bar{X}_l}\right) \tag{24}$$

We know

$$\left| X_2 \frac{P_X}{\overline{X}_l} \right| >$$

$$\Rightarrow c_2 (\overline{X}_l + P_X X_2) < 0$$

As, $\left| X_2 \dfrac{P_l}{X} \right| = \left| \varepsilon_{P_l} \right|$ = elasticity of total marketed surplus with respect to P_l.

$$\left| X_2 \frac{P_X}{X_l} \right| > 1 \Rightarrow \left| \varepsilon_{P_l} \right| > \frac{P_l \overline{X}_l}{P_X X}$$

$$\Rightarrow c_2 \overline{X}_l \left(1 + \frac{P_X X_2}{\overline{X}_l} \right) < 0$$

Thus, if $\left| \varepsilon_{P_l} \right| > \dfrac{P_l \overline{X}_l}{P_X X}$ we can check that using Cramer's rule.

$$\frac{dY}{dP_l} < 0 \text{ and the sign of } \frac{dP_X}{dP_l} > 0 \text{ is indeterminate.}$$

If, however, $\left| X_2 P_X / \overline{X}_l \right| < 1$, we get $dP_X / dP_l > 0$. But, in that case the sign of dY / dP_l is ambiguous. Note that $\left| X_2 P_X / \overline{X}_l \right| < 1$

$$\Rightarrow \left| \varepsilon_{P_l} \right| < \frac{P_l \overline{X}_l}{P_X X}$$

3.3   Reduction in P_r

Differentiating eqn. (6) and (4.11) of the text with respect to P_r we get

$$A_{11} \frac{dY}{dP_r} + A_{12} \frac{dP_X}{dP_r} = X_3^d \tag{25}$$

$$A_{21} \frac{dY}{dP_r} + A_{22} \frac{dP_X}{dP_r} = -\overline{X}_r - P_X X_3^d \tag{26}$$

The signs of $A_{ij}s$ (for $i = 1, 2; j = 1, 2$) are already mentioned above.

The right hand side of eqn. (26) can be written, using relation (4.3) of the text as follows

$$-X_r - P_X X_3^d = -X_r (1 - \alpha) \tag{27}$$

Thus, using Cramer's rule we find that $dP_X / dP_r < 0$, whereas the sign of dY / dP_r is ambiguous.

Notes

1. This model is based on the Rakshit–Taylor framework and is a variant of the Das Model (1987), with some significant differences. The Das model deals with the effects on price and output of the parameters of food policy under three alternative modes of financing the food subsidy, viz. budget deficit, taxation of capitalist's income and levying of excise duty on the industrial output. The budget constraint is not considered here and the subsidy is assumed to be given exogenously. Our model considers levy on the farmers instead of voluntary procurement from the farmers by declaring a procurement price. Das has not considered levy and consequently the marketed surplus function and the associated microfoundations of the two papers are significantly different. Herein lies the importance of this paper.

2. This is actually shown by Das (1987) in the context of her comparative static exercises related to a fall in P_r.

3. This result is also taken from Das (1987). If we consider two time points 1 and 2 the reduction in workers' expenditure which is equivalent to an increase in their income is given by

$$\left\{ \left[P_X\left(X^d - \overline{X}_{r_1}\right) + P_r\,\overline{X}_{r_1} \right] - \left[P_X\left(X^d - \overline{X}_{r_2}\right) + P_r\overline{X}_{r_2} \right] \right\}$$

$$= (P_X - P_r)\,d\overline{X}_r, \text{ where } dX_r \simeq \left(\overline{X}_{r_2} - \overline{X}_{r_1}\right), P_X > P_r$$

4. It is assumed that industrial workers purchase food from the ration shops to meet their subsistence consumption needs and also from the open market in order to meet their above-subsistence purchase plans.

5. $P_X(X - \overline{X}_l) + P_l\overline{X}_l - C(Z) = P_X(Z - X_l) + P_l\overline{X}_l - C(Z) - P_X H$
   is the net income of the farmers i.e., income after excluding the farmer's consumption of food given by $H\,[P_X(Z - \overline{X}_l) + P_l\overline{X}_l - C(Z)]$ which is the gross income the farmers earn by selling food.

6. The various food policy measures which are considered here are the most important ones in this context. There are also other policy measures like increase in food subsidies, which one can check on the basis of our model.

7. If $P_l > P_X$ the farmers will generally sell the entire marketed surplus to the government.

8. This assumption is reasonable in the context of LDCs. The difference between P_l and P_r is financed by the government in the form of subsidies.

9. $(1 - \alpha) > c_2$ implies that the fraction of the increase in income, as a result of an increase in $\overline{X}_r$, which the workers spend on industrial goods is greater than the farmers' marginal propensity to consume industrial goods. See Das (1987).

10. The fact that given $P_X = P^e_X$, the YY curve will shift to the right also implies that the given $Y = Y^e$, P_X will increase.

11. This also implies that given $P_X = P^e{}_X$, Y will fall until the food market equilibrium is reached so that the $X\,X$ curve shifts to the left to $X_2\,X_2$.

12. Here also as a result of an increase in P_l, given $P_X = P^e{}_X$, Y will fall as the $X\,X$ curve shifts upwards to the left.

13. $$\left|\frac{X_2 P_X}{\overline{X}_l}\right| = \left|\frac{X_2 P_X}{\overline{X}_l} \frac{P_l X}{P_l X}\right| = \left|\frac{X_2 P_l}{X} \frac{P_X X}{P_l \overline{X}_l}\right|$$

$$= \left|\frac{X_2 P_l}{X}\right|\left|\frac{P_X X}{P_l \overline{X}_l}\right| = \left|\varepsilon_{P_l}\right|\left|\frac{P_X X}{P_l \overline{X}_l}\right|$$

14. It also implies that given $Y = Y^e$, P_X will fall so that the $Y\,Y$ curve shifts to $Y_1\,Y_1$.

15. Also, given $Y = Y^e$, the fact that the $Y\,Y$ curve shifts to the right implies that P_X will increase.

16. Given $P_X = P^e{}_X$, the fact that the XX curve shifts to $X_1 X_1$ also implies that Y will fall.

17. When $Y\,Y$ shifts to the right to $Y_1\,Y_1$ we can interpret it as that given $Y = Y^e$, P_X will increase.

References

Bose, A. (1985). *Profit and Procurement,* (mimeo). Calcutta: Indian Institute of Management.

——— (1987). Short Period Equilibrium in a Less Developed Economy. In M. Rakshit (ed.) *Studies in the Macroeconomics of Developing Countries,* 26–41. Delhi: Oxford University Press.

Das, C. (1987). Food Policy in a Dual Economy. In *Studies in the Macroeconomics of Developing Countries,* 66–93.

Dasgupta, D. (1988). Procurement Price, Market Price, Employment and Effective Demand. In *Studies in the Macroeconomics of Developing Countries,* 42–65.

George, P.S. (1984). Some aspects of public distribution of foodgrains in India. *Economic and Political Weekly* September 29, Vol. XIX, No. 39 (Review of Agriculture): A106–A110.

Kahlon, A.S. and D.S. Tyagi. (1983) *Agricultural Price Policy in India.* Bombay: Allied Publishers.

Patnaik, P. (1975). Current inflation in India. *Social Scientist* Nos. 30–1: 22–42.

Rakshit, M. (1982). *The Labour Surplus Economy.* Delhi: Macmillan; New Jersey: Humanities Press.

——— (1989). Effective Demand in a Developing Country: Approaches and Issues. In *Studies in the Macroeconomics of Developing Countries,* 1–25.

Taylor, L. (1983). *Structuralist Macro Economics.* New York: Basic Books.

Imported Technologies, Income Distribution and Welfare in the North–South Dialogue

Avanindra N. Bhat[*]

5.1 Introduction

The main issue of the North–South dialogue as seen in current literature is that the South can benefit from importing advanced technologies from the North (see Streeten 1979: 381-400; Helleiner 1977). Batra and Lahiri (1987) have also examined this issue in the context of the mobile capital version of the Harris–Todaro model and concluded

* The author would like to thank A.V.L. Narayana for detailed suggestions in presenting the matter. The author thanks Nadeem Naqvi for pointing out the problem and commenting on earlier drafts. The usual disclaimers apply.

that a greater level of welfare of the South would result from subsidizing the imports of agricultural technology from the North rather than manufacturing technology. Our paper focuses on the impact of importing technologies from the North on the welfare of the South. We are not addressing the issue of how appropriate these technologies are in the developmental efforts of the South, and refrain from the question of substitutability of the existing technologies by the imported ones.[1] Rather, the focus is on the income effects of reduced prices of imported technologies.

In this paper, we use a model of rural–urban migration with inter-sectoral wage differentials that is different from the Harris–Todaro model. The Harris–Todaro model (1970) presumes that migration from agriculture to industry (manufacturing sector) depends upon the perceived probability of a rural migrant finding a job in the industry. In their model, equilibrium is characterised by persistent unemployment in the industry. The Batra–Lahiri model uses this framework. The critical assumption of the Batra–Lahiri model is that wages in the manufacturing sector are rigid, which allow for unemployment in that sector. The wage rate in the agricultural sector is assumed to be flexible enough to clear the labour market. The central conclusion of this model is that concessions on imports of agricultural technology would improve the welfare of the South more than such similar concessions would on industrial technology.

In this paper we consider a two-sector small economy framework in the importing country as in Batra and Lahiri (1987). But, we change their assumption of labour union pressure on industrial wages and allow for wage-flexibility in the industrial sector. In agriculture we assume, like in the Lewis model (1954), that labour supply is unlimited (perfectly elastic) and wages are flexible. Thus, at a given wage rate, there will be an infinite supply forthcoming. The amount of labour employed is determined by the demand-side marginal productivity conditions. Thus, agricultural unemployment is due to excess labour supply. In industry, however, the labour supply curve is assumed to be upward sloping, reflecting supply constraints that exist due to costs of acquiring skills. When labour demand curves are downward sloping the above stated assumptions in both the sectors imply that, in equilibrium, there is unemployment in agriculture and full employment in manufacturing. Under these assumptions, it will be shown that in the case of both industry and agriculture, the impact of subsidised imported technologies on the welfare of the South is ambiguous, unlike in the Batra and Lahiri model. In Batra and Lahiri

(1987), agricultural technology was shown to be always superior to manufacturing technology in terms of an income gain for the South. This is not the case in our paper. One of the main conclusions that we have arrived at is that, as far as import benefits to the South are concerned, whether or not the agricultural technology is superior (or inferior) to the industrial technology would depend on the sectoral elasticities of equilibrium labour demand.

The following Section presents the model briefly, while Section 5.3 discusses the impact of subsidies for imported technologies in each sector on national income. Issues relating to income distribution are discussed in Section 5.4 and conclusions stated in Section 5.5.

5.2   The Model

Our model is similar to the two-sector model (agriculture and manufacturing) as discussed in Batra and Lahiri (1987) with certain modifications in labour markets. First, in product markets in the two sectors, we assume that the production functions are concave and linearly homogeneous. Hence for agriculture:

$$A = A(K_a, L_a, Z_a) = L_a\, a(k_a, z_a) \tag{5.1}$$

for manufacturing:

$$M = M(K_m, L_m, Z_m) = L_m\, m(k_m, z_m) \tag{5.2}$$

where, K_i is the capital stock in the ith sector, L_i is the amount of labour employed in equilibrium in the ith sector and Z_i is the sector-specific imported technology in the ith sector; k_i and z_i are the capital/labour ratio and the technology/labour ratio, $i = a, m$. The average labour productivities in agriculture and manufacturing are $a(.)$ and $m(.)$ respectively.

The capital market equilibrium obtains when

$$a_k(k_a, z_a) = r, \tag{5.3a}$$

$$m_k(k_m, z_m) = r \tag{5.3b}$$

where r is the rental for capital services, a_k and a_z are the marginal products in the agricultural sector with respect to k_a, z_a and m_k, m_z, are the corresponding marginal products in the manufacturing sector. Equations (5.3a, 5.3b) follow from the assumption that capital is perfectly mobile between the two sectors, making the rental rates in the two sectors equal. Without loss of generality, the constant relative price of M in terms of A is assumed to be unity.

5.2.1 Labour markets

The labour market assumptions of our model are as follows. On account of an unlimited supply of labour, the labour supply curve is assumed to be perfectly elastic with respect to the real wage rate in agriculture, whereas it is assumed to be upward sloping in industry due to the costs of skill acquisition. The labour demand curves in both the sectors are assumed to be downward sloping and are given by the marginal productivities of labour ($MP_{L\,a}$, $MP_{L\,m}$). The Batra–Lahiri model assumed wage-flexibility and therefore full employment equilibrium in agriculture. They assumed wage-rigidity in industry to reflect pressures from labour unions and, consequently assumed unemployment in equilibrium in that sector. In contrast, we assume that there is unemployment in agriculture, like in the Lewis model due to an unlimited labour supply. In industry however, we relax the wage-rigidity assumption and consider the situation of full employment. Thus, we make a departure from the Batra–Lahiri model. This would also allow us to examine the implications of technology import subsidies on the welfare of the importing country under a different set of labour market assumptions. The equilibrium amount of labour is determined by the usual marginal productivity condition in the two sectors as given below.

$$w_a = MP_{La} = a - a_k k_a - z_a a_z, \tag{5.4}$$

$$w_m = MP_{Lm} = m - m_k k_m - z_m m_z, \tag{5.5}$$

where w_i is the real wage in sector i and is obtained by using the intensive production function assumed in the present model (we use these expressions without proof).

Further, a wage differential is assumed to persist between the two sectors and without loss of generality, we assume that the manufacturing wage is higher than the agricultural wage:

$$w_m = w_a + \alpha, \alpha \; 0. \tag{5.6}$$

α is endogenously determined in this model so that the wage differential gets determined within the model. This condition implies that there will be rural-to-urban migration of labour, which tends to ease supply constraints in the labour market in the manufacturing sector. The imported technologies being sector specific are however immobile between the two sectors. Each sector tends to import technologies up to the point where their marginal productivity equals their respective real royalty rate (ρ_i). The international prices of technologies, ρ_i^* are assumed to be given and held constant. The Southern economy assumed to be small is a price taker and its real royalty rate differs from ρ_i^* by the amount of subsidy. Hence, in equilibrium,

$$a_z(k_a, z_a) = \rho_a = (1 - s_a) \rho_a^*, \tag{5.7}$$

$$m_z(k_m, z_m) = \rho_m = (1 - s_m) \rho_{m*} \tag{5.8}$$

where s_a, s_m are the respective subsidy rates given for the two sectors.[2]

The standard conditions on the production functions and their marginal products as given in (A.1) and (A.2) (See Appendix 1), in Batra and Lahiri (1987: 29) are assumed to be satisfied in our analysis as well. Agricultural unemployment is represented by U. The total labour supply L in the economy is given by:

$$L_a + L_m + U = \overline{L}, \tag{5.9}$$

$\overline{K}$ is the total supply of capital given by:

$$K_a + K_m = L_a k_a + L_m k_m = \overline{K}. \tag{5.10}$$

Unemployment in the economy is assumed to be a function of the wage differential. As U increases, α decreases. This is because the wage differential α plays the same role as e in Batra and Lahiri (1987), the probability of finding a job in the manufacturing sector. There, $e = Lm / (Lm + U)$. Here, α is the incremental wage rate in the manufacturing sector that depends on the unemployment rate in the agricultural sector. The smaller U is, the larger would be α because the probability of a migrant finding a job is higher and vice versa. Thus, we assume that

$$U = g(\alpha). \tag{5.11}$$

Real national income of the South is given by

$$Y = A + M - \rho_a Z_a - \rho_m Z_m = w_a L_a + w_m L_m + r\overline{K}. \tag{5.12}$$

This completes the model specification of the small open Southern economy. Equations 5.3a, 5.3b, 5.4, 5.5, 5.6, 5.7, 5.8, 5.9, 5.10 and 5.11 are the ten equations which determine the ten endogenous variables namely w_a, w_m, k_a, k_m, z_m, z_a, L_a, L_m, U and α; the parameters of interest in the system are r, ρ_a, ρ_m, $\overline{L}$ and $\overline{K}$. For a detailed solution of the model, see Appendix 1.

5.3   Varying Royalty Rates and National Income of the South

As the focus of this paper is the issue of subsidising imported technologies, a natural policy question would be to study the impact of such concessions in the form of reduced royalty rates on the welfare of the South. Welfare considerations are captured by the real national income of the economy. Real national income Y of the South can be written as

$$Y = w_m \overline{L} - \alpha L_a - w_m U + r\overline{K}$$

using the fact that $w_m = w_a + \alpha$.
On totally differentiating this expression for Y, we get:

$$dY = \overline{L}\, dw_m - d\,(\alpha L_a) - d\,(w_m U). \tag{5.13}$$

First, we will study the impact of a change in the royalty rate of imported agricultural technology on the national income (in the absence of any subsidies). Thus,

$$\frac{dY}{d\rho_a} = -\frac{d\,(\alpha L_a)}{d\rho_a} - w_m \frac{dU}{d\rho_a}$$

This follows from the results shown in Appendix 1 which are:

$$\frac{dw_a}{d\rho a} = -z_a, \frac{dr}{d\rho a} = 0, \frac{dw_m}{d\rho a} = 0.$$

On substituting these values,

$$\frac{dY}{d\rho a} = -z_a L_a + \alpha z_a (dL_a / dw_a) + z_a w_m g_2,$$

where $g_2 = (dU / dwa)$.
Further, the same expression can be rewritten as

$$\frac{dY}{d\rho a} = -z_a L_a (1 - \in_a) - w_m z_a (dL_m / dw_a)$$

where $\in a = -(w_a / L_a)\,(dL_a / dw_a)$ is the elasticity of equilibrium labour demand in agriculture. Similarly, the impact of ρ_m on Y is given by

$$\frac{dY}{d\rho m} = -Z_m L_m (1 - \in_m) - w_a z_m \frac{dL_a}{dw_m}$$

See Appendix 1, where $\in_m = - (w_m / L_m) (dL_m / dw_m)$ is the elasticity of equilibrium labour demand in the manufacturing sector.

5.3.1 Labour mobility across sectors

Now, $\bar{L} = L_m + L_a + U$ where U is the level of unemployment in the economy. Thus,

$$\frac{dL_m}{dw_a} + \frac{dL_a}{dw_a} + \frac{dU}{dw_a} = 0$$

so that

$$\frac{dL_m}{dw_a} = \frac{dL_a}{dw_a} + \frac{dU}{dw_a}.$$

On account of imported technology in agriculture, there will be an increase in labour productivity, or a rightward shift in the labour demand curve. This also implies a higher level of employment for the same wage rate or a higher wage for the same level of employment within agriculture or a mixture of both these effects. However, because of the wage differential, the level of unemployment is likely to decrease in agriculture partly due to migration of labour to the manufacturing sector. It follows that

$$\frac{dU}{dw_a} < 0, \quad \frac{dL_a}{dw_a} < 0 \quad \text{and} \quad \frac{dL_m}{dw_a} > 0.$$

The model only considers those cases for which $\dfrac{dL_a}{dw_a} < 0$.

This would imply that when imported technology shifts the productivity schedule in the agricultural sector, this shift is smaller than the wage rate increase implying a decrease in agricultural employment (L_a). However, on account of migration some workers are absorbed in the manufacturing sector, and total unemployment decreases. Other cases could be easily discussed but we feel that this is the realistic case. Imported technologies, it is felt, will displace labour and not augment it.

Similarly, as w_m increases, perhaps due to the use of imported manufacturing technology, there will be a rightward shift in the labour demand curve but not as much as the increase in w_m and the equilibrium level of employment decreases in the manufacturing sector. However the amount of labour employed in agriculture is unaffected so that

$$\frac{dL_a}{dw_m} = 0, \quad \frac{dL_m}{dw_m} < 0 \quad \text{and} \quad \frac{dU}{dw_m} > 0.$$

Further,

$$\frac{dY}{d\rho_m} = -z_m L_m (1 - \in_m)$$

and

$$\frac{dY}{d\rho_a} = -z_a L_a (1 - \in_a) - w_m z_a \frac{dL_m}{dw_a}.$$

Now, $\frac{dY}{d\rho a}$ could be alternatively written as

$$\frac{dY}{d\rho a} = -z_a L_a - w_a z_a \frac{dL_a}{dw_a} - w_m z_a \frac{dL_m}{dw_a}.$$

By our assumption, $\frac{dL_a}{dw_a} > 0$,

and as before, $\frac{dL_a}{dw_a} < 0$.

The comparison of the two sectoral impacts is summarized in Theorem 1.

Theorem 1:

(a) *Reductions* in the royalty rates of imported agricultural technologies will *increase* the real national income of the South

$$\frac{dY}{d\rho a} < 0 \quad \text{if} \quad 0 < \in_a < 1.$$

(b) The impact of subsidies in manufacturing technology on income is expressed by:

$$\frac{dY}{d\rho m} > 0 \quad \text{if} \quad \in_m > 1,$$

$$\frac{dY}{d\rho m} < 0 \text{ if } 0 < \in_m < 1,$$

that is, concessions in the form of a *lower* royalty rate on imported industrial technology will *lower* or *increase* the real national income of the South depending on the magnitude of $\in_m$. Further, two possible cases could arise when $0 < \in_m 1,$:

i) $\in_a < \in_m$: $\left| \frac{1}{Z_a} \frac{dY}{d\rho a} \right| > \left| \frac{1}{Z_m} \frac{dY}{d\rho m} \right|$

ii) $\in_a > \in_m$: $\left| \frac{1}{Z_a} \frac{dY}{d\rho a} \right| > \left| \frac{1}{Z_m} \frac{dY}{d\rho m} \right|$

if $\dfrac{\in_{m.a}}{(\in_a - \in_m) + \in_{m.a}} > k$ where $\in_{m.a} = \dfrac{w_a}{L_m} \dfrac{dL_m}{dw_a}$ and

$$k = \frac{w_a L_a}{w_a L_a + w_m L_m}$$

Proof: The proofs follow immediately on substituting for

$$\frac{dY}{d\rho a}, \quad \frac{dY}{d\rho m}$$

Results summarized in this proposition are obtained using the framework of inter-industry wage differentials in contrast to the mobile capital version of the Harris–Todaro model employed by Batra and Lahiri (1987). To that extent, our results are different from the conclusions arrived at in the earlier work.

In Theorem 1, we present a scenario where concessions obtained by the South on importing agricultural technologies from the North are seen to be very powerful in improving the welfare of the South if $0 < \in_a < 1$; whereas concessions on imported technology in industry may *not* always improve the welfare of the South as is the case with agriculture. It should be emphasised that our results depend on the sector specific elasticities of equilibrium labour demand. It is different from the corresponding result in Batra and Lahiri (1987) in that the direction of the impact of a change in ρ_m on Y_m or ρ_a on Y_a depends on the sectoral labour elasticity in equilibrium ($\in_m$) or ($\in_a$).

Furthermore, whether the impact would be favourable or not depends on $\in_m$ or $\in_a$. Cases (i) and (ii) above compare the two impacts when an equivalent decrease in the two royalties is made, (that is, $Z_a\, d\, \rho_a = Z_m\, d\, \rho_m$) where the terms on the left-hand side and the right-hand side of this equation are the total value of concessions made by the North (or equivalently, the subsidy granted by the South). In case (i) for $\in_m < \in_a$, equivalent reductions made in the total value of concessions raise the national income more in the case of agricultural technology than in the case of manufacturing technology. In case (ii) for $\in_a > \in_m$, the same result would hold only if the condition given in Theorem (1) on the sectoral equilibrium labour elasticities is met. Using econometric methods given data, $\in_a$, $\in_m$, $\in_{m.a}$ and k, can be estimated. We could check these conditions to identify which sector has a greater impact on real income. This would be important from the policy point of view.

Let us briefly discuss the labour demand elasticities. Suppose the labour demand and labour supply equations are

$$L_D = \alpha + \beta w + \in_1 \text{ and}$$

$$L_s = \tau + \delta w + \in_2.$$

Identification in such a system would proceed with the assumption that the variance of the first equation is significantly less than the variance of the second equation. This would imply that supply shifts would more or less occur along the demand line and hence the locus of equilibrium points is negatively sloped. Such an elasticity of this mongrel equation is distinct from the usual supply elasticity or the demand elasticity.

5.4   Income Distribution

In this section, the focus is on the income distribution of the South and how it changes with respect to the royalty rates of imported technologies. Let W represent the total wage income. Then,

$$W = w_a\, L_a + w_m\, L_m,$$

$$= w_m\, \overline{L} - w_m\, U - \alpha L_a \text{, using the wage differential equation}$$

$$w_m = w_a + \alpha \text{ and } L_a + L_m + U = \overline{L}.$$

Let β be the share of labour in national income. Then, we can express β as follows:

$\beta = (W/Y)$.

Furthermore,

$$\frac{d\beta}{d\rho a} = \frac{Y\frac{dW}{d\rho a} - w\frac{dY}{d\rho a}}{Y^2} = \frac{1}{Y}\frac{dY}{d\rho a} - \frac{W}{Y^2}\frac{dY}{d\rho a}.$$

Now,

$$\frac{dY}{d\rho a} = \frac{dW}{d\rho a} \text{ because } r\overline{K} \text{ is fixed.}$$

Therefore,

$$\frac{d\beta}{d\rho a} = \frac{1}{Y^2}\frac{dY}{d\rho a}(Y - W) = \frac{r\overline{K}}{Y^2}\frac{dY}{d\rho a}$$

Thus,

$$\frac{d\beta}{d\rho a} = \frac{r\overline{K}}{Y^2}\frac{dY}{d\rho a}$$

Thus,

$$\text{sign}\left(\frac{d\beta}{d\rho a}\right) = \text{sign}\left(\frac{dY}{d\rho a}\right),$$

and as seen before,

$$\frac{d\beta}{d\rho a} < 0 \text{ 0 since } \frac{dY}{d\rho a} < 0 \text{ if } 0 < \in_a < 1.$$

On similar lines, $(d\beta / d\rho_m)$ is computed as

$$\frac{d\beta}{d\rho m} = \frac{r\overline{k}}{Y^2}\frac{dY}{d\rho m}$$

Thus, $\text{sign}\left(\dfrac{d\beta}{d\rho m}\right) = \text{sign}\left(\dfrac{dY}{d\rho m}\right)$

We summarize these results in the following proposition.

Theorem 2:

(a) *Decreases* in the royalty rate on imported agricultural technology would favourably affect the income distribution of wage earners, that is,

$$\frac{d\beta}{d\rho a} < 0 \text{ if } 0 < \in_a < 1.$$

(b) *Decreases* in the royalty rate on imported manufacturing technology would favourably affect the income distribution of wage earners, only if $0 < \in_m < 1$, that is

$$\frac{d\beta}{d\rho m} > 0 \text{ if } \in_m > 1 \text{ and } \frac{d\beta}{d\rho m} < 0 \text{ if } 0 < \in_m < 1.$$

5.5 Conclusion

The wage differential approach pursued here alters the North–South dialogue and the issues involved. This paper uses the same framework suggested in an earlier paper by Batra and Lahiri (1987) but reaches different conclusions. Adoption of imported technology in agriculture can increase the share of wage earners in the South, whereas in industry it may or may not do so depending on $\in_a$, $\in_m$. Technology imports into the industrial sector can favourably influence the welfare in the South only if the elasticity of equilibrium labour demand in industry is less than unity. This in turn, has a bearing on the subsidies allowed for technology imports. The policy implications of the results derived in this paper may provide useful signals to any developing economy, given the empirical values of labour elasticities discussed above for the agriculture and manufacturing sectors. As no recent estimates of these elasticities are available for India, it is not possible to support or negate the governments' policy neutrality *vis-à-vis* imported technology between the agricultural and the manufacturing sectors.

Appendix 1

In this appendix, we derive the dependence of the real wage rate (w_a) on the royalty rates ρ_a and ρ_m. We will assume that the subsidies are ignored.

We begin by considering the equation,

$$w_a = a - k_a a_k - z_a a_z.$$

This can be rewritten as

$$w_a L_a = A - K_a a_k - Z_a a_z.$$

Totally differentiating this equation,

$$w_a\, dL_a + L_a\, dw_a = (A_K\, dK_a + A_L\, dL_a + A_Z\, dZ_a) - a_k\, dK_a$$
$$- K_a (da_k) - Z_a\, da_z - a_z\, dZ_a.$$

From the production function conditions,

$$A_K = a_k,\ A_Z = a_z = \rho_a^* = \rho_a,\ \text{and } A_L = w_a$$

so that $L_a\, dw_a = - K_a a_{kk}\, dk_a - K_a a_{kz}\, dz_a - Z_a\, d\rho_a.$

This can be rewritten as

$$L_a\, dw_a = - K_a\, da_k - Z_a\, d\rho_a, = - K_a\, dr - Z_a\, d\rho_a.$$

Thus, $dw_a = - k_a\, dr - z_a\, d\rho_a.$ (A.1)

This shows that $w_a = w_a\,(r,\, \rho_a)$. Thus,

$$\frac{dw_a}{d\rho a} = - z_a \quad \text{and} \quad \frac{dw_a}{dr} = - k_a. \quad\quad\text{(A.2)}$$

Also, since r does not depend on $\rho_a,\, \rho_m,$

$$\frac{dr}{d\rho a} = 0 = \frac{dr}{d\rho m}. \quad\quad\text{(A.3)}$$

[(A.1) – (A.3) are used in Sections 5.3 and 5.4 of the paper.]
On similar lines, we can show that

$$\frac{dw_m}{d\rho m} = - z_m.$$

We already have $dY = \bar{L}\, dw_m - d(\alpha L_a) - d(w_m U)$. On expanding the differentials and substituting for α, U and noting that $dwa\, /\, d\rho_m = 0$, we have the following equation:

$$\frac{dY}{d\rho m} = L_m\frac{dw_m}{d\rho m} + w_m\frac{dL_m}{d\rho m} + w_a\frac{dL_a}{d\rho m}$$

$$= - z_m L_m - z_m w_m\frac{dL_m}{dw_m} - z_m w_a\frac{dL_a}{dw_m}$$

$$= - z_m L_m (1 - \in_m) - z_m w_a\frac{dL_a}{dw_m}.$$

Notes

1. These issues are addressed in Helleiner (1977: 305–307), Streeten (1979: 381–400). As excellently stated by Helleiner (1977): Apart from the prices paid by the developing countries for technology imports, the other principal issue is the "appropriateness" of imported technologies to local physical, economic, and social environments. These two issues of prices and quality are interrelated since the lowering of the relative price of unsuitable technology may, through undesirable substitution effects, generate socially perverse results.

2. In India, for instance, under the liberalization policy introduced in 1991, the transfer of foreign technology is permitted in selected priority areas, including agro-based products, agricultural machinery, etc., but, no preferential tax treatment is accorded to agriculture overmanufacturing. In either case, the royalty paid for imported technologies is tax-exempt, while there are restrictions on the extent of royalty that can be paid to the suppliers.

References

Batra, R. N. and S. Lahiri. (1987). Imported Technology, Urban Employment and the North–South Dialogue. *Journal of Development Economics* 25: 21–32.

Helleiner, G.K. (1977). International Technology Issues: Southern Needs and Northern Responses. In *The New International Economic Order: The North–South Debate*, ed. J.N. Bhagwati, Chap. 12. Cambridge, Mass.: MIT Press.

Lewis, W.A. (1954). Economic Development with Unlimited Supplies of Labour. *The Manchester School*, 28.

Neary, J. (1981). In the Harris–Todaro Model with Intersectoral Capital Mobility. *Economica* 48: 219–234.

O.E.C.D. (1981). *North–South Technology Transfer: The Adjustment Ahead.* Paris.

Streeten, P. (1979). Technology Gaps Between the Rich and the Poor Countries. In *The Frontiers of Development Studies*, ed. P. Streeten, 381–400. London: Macmillan.

Subcontracting, Subsidized Credit and the Informal Sector

Malabika Roy

6.1 Introduction

Outside the organized economy, almost in every country, and specially in less developed countries, there exists an informal sector which provides employment to a large section of the population. 'Informal sector' is a blanket term used to cover varied activities which do not come under the aegis of the organized production structure. Broadly, it can be divided into a production subsector and a service subsector.

The informal service sector is engaged in providing various informal services to the consumers. The informal production subsector, on the other hand, is engaged in the production of material goods. Sometimes, a production unit may combine both the operations. Informal production units can be independent producers serving a low income market, but often a production link exists between the formal and informal units. This paper is concerned with this latter aspect.

In simple terms, subcontracting means farming out a part or whole of the production of a commodity to a smaller production unit by a bigger firm (usually called a parent firm), which has an independent identity. Prevalence of subcontracting relations between the formal and informal sector has been emphasized in a number of studies. The studies by Bose (1978), Romatate (1983), Harris (1982), and Nagraj (1984), have focused upon the exploitative relation resulting from this kind of unequal dependence. Watanabe (1971) has discussed at length the various forms that subcontracting can take, and the reasons for its coming into existence. According to Watanabe as well as Nagraj, one of the major reasons for its growth in less developed countries is the duality in the labour market.

In today's world, modern industrial growth is spreading from the developed countries to the developing countries. Along with the growth of industries, an organised labour movement has also grown. As a result, a firm operating in the formal sector faces an organised labour force which has some degree of bargaining power. This bargaining power is partly supported by the prevalent political and administrative structure, and partly by various entry requirements maintained by the formal sector units, which often ensure a better quality of labour. Hence the labour cost is higher in the formal sector than in the informal sector. Outside the more fortunate working population employed by the formal sector a vast unemployed labour force exists, willing to work at a lower wage, which the organized industries cannot absorb. The informal units can take advantage of this residual labour force. Also, these small units not being a part of the organized economy do not come under the scope of the laws that protect the organised sector labour force. Even if any legislation exists, it is safely ignored, as enforcement of these laws is almost impossible given the amorphous structure of the informal sector.

The informal units also enjoy some other advantages. They have smaller overhead costs. Sometimes their production cost is lower because they use labour intensive methods. (Capital is expensive in less developed economies compared to labour). So the commodities that have perfect, or near perfect, divisible production processes can be produced by the informal sector at a much lower cost.

Informal units find the subcontracting arrangement profitable because their marketing capacity is usually very limited. They also have inadequate access to the source of funds available in the organized credit market. The prerequisites of and the paraphernalia involved in obtaining credit from the organized credit market are so elaborate and time consuming that the informal sector is deterred from depending on organized credit. The parent firm can provide the informal sector with a market, and any other assistance necessary, which may include supply of finance, supply of a scarce input or technological expertise. In return the informal sector helps the formal sector to make use of the unorganized labour force to which the formal sector does not have direct access.

The recent years have seen a lot of interest in the activities of the informal sector due to their employment generating capacity. Small scale production units also form a part of the informal sector. Policies have been laid down to help these units. A major proposition is the provision of credit for production purposes at a subsidized rate of interest. However, these broad policy measures have failed to take into account the specific set up in which a particular informal unit may be working. Especially, its links with the formal sector, and the circumstances that have given rise to this type of linkage have been ignored. This paper considers a situation where the lack of marketing channels is a more fundamental problem with the informal units than credit constraint. As long as the formal producer remains the only, or major marketing outlet, the informal units may prefer not to avail of the credit facility. Alternatively, if the loan is taken, it may become unproductive, that is, the output may fall as a consequence. It is also shown that supply of subsidized credit can generate a higher level of production only when the formal sector producer can utilize the credit to reap additional profits while restricting the informal units to their reservation income. If such is the case it is equivalent, or, better to give the credit directly to the formal sector.

In the first part of the paper we start with the assumption that the formal sector producer is the sole source of finance to the informal units. The formal producer borrows from the organised credit market and advances the money to the informal units. He does not face any credit constraint in the organized credit market. In the second part, credit constraint in the organized credit market for the formal sector is introduced. In each case, the effect of allowing the informal units to borrow from the organized credit market at a subsidized rate of interest is then analysed.

6.2 The Model

The theory of interlinked contracts has been widely studied with reference to developing economies to explain the operation of rural credit markets. The idea of such an interlinked dual pricing system

originally came from a paper by Oi (1971). The idea behind interlinked contracts is that when an agent operates in two markets
simultaneously, he can exploit his borrower far more than if he was
operating in only one market. Some of the important papers in this
field are Bardhan (1980), Basu (1983), Gangopadhyay and Sengupta
(1987), Roy and Sengupta (1989). I have used the idea of interlinked
contract to capture the process of subcontracting. The model is
described in the following paragraphs.

The industry can be subdivided into a formal sector and an informal
sector. The formal sector producer is assumed to be a monopoly.[1] There
are n informal sector producers working under him as subcontractors.
The output x can either be produced within the informal sector or within
the formal sector. Without going into the details of comparative cost
advantage it is assumed that the cost of producing the output is lower
in the informal sector units than in the formal sector.[2]

We consider an extreme situation where the informal units do not
have access to the final goods market. Their only marketing outlet is
the formal sector. The formal sector concentrates all its resources in
marketing activities. It enjoys the benefits of an established brand
name and supplies a whole range of commodities in the market, of
which x is one. It is also assumed that though the sales and marketing
network is common, production and sales of x is not affected by—and
does not—affect the sale of any other commodity produced and
marketed by this firm. Hence, the profit for this commodity can be
calculated separately. Examples of such subcontracting can be found
in Basu (1977a, 1977b). In the next four sections, a model of formal
sector–informal sector linkage is developed, and the impact of easy
credit policy towards the informal sector is examined under alternative
assumptions.

6.3   Effect of Subsidized Credit with Given
        Number of Informal Units

Let A be the monopolist formal sector producer, and let $\bar{n}$ be the
number of informal units producing for him. $\bar{n}$ is assumed to be given,
as producer A has contact with $\bar{n}$ units only. The informal units do
not have access to any funds. Producer A borrows from the organised
credit market and lends the funds to the informal units.[3]

Producer A and the informal sector producers are profit
maximizers. Producer A determines the price at which he is going to

buy the output x from the informal units and the interest rate he is going to charge on the fund advanced. The inferior bargaining position of the informal units is reflected in their accepting the price offered by A per unit of output as well as the interest rate charged. Their decision making is limited to the quantity to be supplied while operating as price takers. Each individual informal producer has a reservation income that he can earn elsewhere, and he will have to be ensured of at least as much as that if he is to act as a subcontractor. It is also assumed that all the informal units have an identical cost structure and the same reservation income.

Given the above assumptions, the profit function of the ith informal unit is given by :

$$\pi_i = P_i x_i - (1 + r_i) C(x_i) \; i = 1, \dots n \tag{6.1}$$

where P_i is the price offered by producer A to the ith informal unit; r_i is the interest charged by A from the ith informal unit; and $C(x_i)$ is the cost of producing x_i units of output. This cost function is assumed to be identical for all the $\overline{n}$ informal units. It has the following properties : $C'(x_i) > 0, C''(x) \geq 0$, with all the higher order derivatives being positive or zero, $C'(0) \simeq 0$.

The amount of x_i the subcontractor is ready to supply at each price is given by :

$$P_i = (1 + r_i) C'(x_i) \; i = 1, \dots n \tag{6.2}$$

There is also the additional condition π_i must satisfy to make subcontracting possible :

$$\pi_i \geq W_r \tag{6.3}$$

where W_r is the reservation income which is the same for all units. The inverse demand function facing producer A is given by :

$$P = P(X_A) \; p'(X_A) < 0, \tag{6.4}$$

where X_A is the total output sold by the firm, $X_A = \sum_i^n x_i$.

The total revenue function for producer A is

$$R = P(X_A) X_A$$

The demand function satisfies the following properties

$$dR / dX_A > 0; \; d^2R / dX^2_A < 0.$$

The profit function for the formal sector can be written as :

$$\prod_A^m = P(X_A)X_A - (1+r^*)\sum_i C(x_i)$$

$$- \sum \{p_i x_i - (1+r_i)\, C\,(x_i)\} \tag{6.5}$$

where, $X_A = \sum x_i$, r^* : the rate of interest prevailing in the organized credit market.

Proposition 6.1: If $(1 + r^*_i, p^*_i)$ is the optimal contract, then $P^*_i\, x^*_i - (1 + r^*_i)\, C(x_i) = W_r$.

Proof: If $P_i\, x_i - (1 + r)\, C_i(x_i) > W_r$, then producer A will be able to do better by reducing π_is, thereby increasing his own profit $\prod_m^A$ as is clear from equation (6.5). As long as he is controlling both P^*_i and $1 + r^*_i$, he can reduce π_i, by reducing both proportionally. From equation (6.2) it is clear that a proportional reduction of $(P_i, 1 + r_i)$ will not affect the level of supply. Thus, he can ensure that the informal units always get their reservation incomes only, without disturbing the supply of output.[4]

Hence,

$$P^*_i\, x_i - (1 + r^*_i)\, C\,(x_i) = W_r. \tag{6.6}$$

As long as producer A has control over both price and rate of interest, borrowing the term from Basu (1984, 1986) we can say that he will act as an all or nothing monopolist. By appropriately choosing $(P_i, 1 + r_i)$ producer A can confine the informal units to their reservation incomes.

Producer A's profit function then takes the form:

$$\prod_m^A = P\,(X_A)\, X_A - (1 + r^*)\sum_i C(x_i) - \bar{n} W_r |1|$$

The profit maximizing choice of x_i for producer A is obtained from the condition:

$$MR_A = P\,(X_A) + X_A P'\,(X_A) = (1 + r^*)\, C'\,(x_i) \tag{6.7}$$

Given identical cost functions, and the same level of reservation income for all informal sector units, $x_i = \bar{x}_m$ for all i, and, $P_i = P_m$, $r_i = r_m$. This will also be true for all future analysis. Henceforth we will treat $x_i = x$ to be the same for all $\bar{n}$ units. Total output is $X^{-m}_A = \bar{n} x_m$.

Now let us consider the effect of the government policy of providing loans to the informal units at a rate of interest $r^{**} \leq r^*$ through the banking sector. This also implies that the process of obtaining credit has been simplified to make the organised sector loans more accessible to the informal units. Now producer A no longer has the two variables within his control. How the formal sector–informal sector relation will be affected depends on the distribution of bargaining power between the two groups, and the loss each party experiences if the other party refuses to cooperate. For instance, if the formal sector producer is strong enough to determine unilaterally both the level of output ordered from the informal units and the purchase price of this output, as long as equation (6.3) is satisfied, he will corner all the gains from a lower rate of interest. He will order his profit-maximizing level of output and fix p in such a way that the informal units are just ensured of W_r. The supply function given by equation (6.2) will then become invalid.

The underlying assumption in Section 6.1 is that the informal units carry out a profit-maximizing exercise of their own, rather than passively accepting the total amount that producer A is ready to pay them. That is why producer A needs control over the interest rate as well as the price to drive the informal units down to their reservation incomes. Condition (6.2) operates as a lower limit to the acceptable levels of income rather than as a basis of bargaining. Also, if the loss of the formal sector producer A is large enough in case the informal units refuse to produce for him, his bargaining position will be substantially weaker.

So the same process of price formation and income determination as earlier is retained for the informal units even after they have access to organized credit. The underlying bargaining process that generates such a structure is not elaborated upon. Since the informal units still do not have any marketing outlet other than producer A, while producer A can produce the commodity himself, this asymmetry is assumed to result in the formal sector still being the market leader.

In the altered state, producer A only determines the price he is willing to pay, and the informal units determine the quantity they are willing to supply at each price. The profit function of individual informal units are given by

$$\pi_i = P_i x_i - C(x_i)(1 + r^{**}) \tag{6.1a}$$

Profit maximization yields the supply function:

$$P_i = (1 + r^{**})\, C'\,(x_i) \qquad\qquad (6.2a)$$

Producer A now faces the profit function:

$$\prod_{A}^{m} = P(X_A)X_A - \sum_{i}^{n} p_i X_i \qquad\qquad (6.8)$$

He maximizes his profit taking into account equation (6.2a). Profit maximizing behaviour on his part yields the following condition:

$$MR_A = P(X_A) + X_A P'(X_A) = (1 + r^{**})[C'(X)] \qquad (6.7a)$$

For $r^{**} = r^*$, the output will obviously fall below $\overline{nx_m}$. Comparing eqn. (6.7a) with eqn. (6.7) we can see that the curve $(1 + r^{**})$ $[C'(x) + xC''(x)]$ lies above the marginal cost curve $(1 + r^*)C'(x)$, while the marginal revenue curve remains unaltered. (See Fig. 6.1).

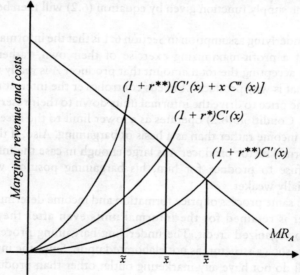

Fig. 6.1

For $r^{**} < r^*$, we show in the following section that the profit-maximizing output of the monopolist will be lower than $\overline{nx_m}$ if certain conditions prevail:

Proposition 6.2: If $r^* \leq 1$, and $r^{**} > 0$, the output will always fall.

Proof: Let us construct a function:

$$L = (1 + r^*)\, C''(x) - (1 + r^{**})\,[2C''(x) + xC^{3}(x)]$$

where $(1 + r^*)C''(x)$: slope of the function $(1 + r^*)C'(x)$.

$(1 + r^{**})[2C''(x) + xC^3(x)]$:

slope of the function $(1 + r^{**})[C'(x) + xC''(x)]$
Rearranging the terms:

$$L = (1 + r^{**}) \left[\frac{r^* - r^{**}}{1 + r^{**}} - 1 \right] c''(x) - (1 + r^{**})xc^3(x)$$

Given $r^* \leq 1$, $r^{**} > 0$, $L < 0$ for all $x \geq 0$.

In other words, the curve $(1 + r^*)C'(x)$ will lie above $(1 + r^{**})$ $[C'(x) + xC''(x)]$, if the conditions mentioned above are satisfied. Given the same revenue function output will always fall.

Let the solution to the system be $(\widetilde{p}, \widetilde{x})$.

The reason behind this fall in the size of the profit maximizing demand lies in the changing role of producer A. When he was acting as an all or nothing monopolist he made sure that none of the surplus went to the informal units. The conditions $P_m / C'(x_m) = (1 + r_m)$ implies that the price he pays for the proceeds from one unit of loan is exactly equal to the return in terms of rate of interest on advance plus the advance itself. The cost of producing an extra unit is then just $(1 + r^*)C'(x_m)$. So the producer gives an order of size $\bar{x}_m$, such that, $MR_A = (1 + r^*)C'(\bar{x}_m)$.

When the informal units can borrow from the organized credit market, producer A can no longer prevent the informal units from getting a part of the surplus, as he can no longer confine them to the level of reservation income by controlling both price and the rate of interest. Now, $p(\widetilde{x}) = (1 + r^{**})C'(\widetilde{x})$, and, the marginal cost of buying an extra unit is $p(\widetilde{x}) > \widetilde{x}P'(\widetilde{x})\lambda + (1 + r^*)C'(\widetilde{x})$ for $r^{**} = r^*$. For $r^{**} < r^*$, there are two effects, $p(x) < (1 + r^*)C'(x)$, but, $p(x) + xp(x)$ may or may not be greater than $(1 + r^*)C'(x)$. The lower rate of interest reduces the purchase price below the previous marginal cost, thus tending to increase the order, while the monopolistic element tends to reduce the order. $r^* \leq 1$ and $r^{**} > 0$, give the sufficient limits within which the second effect is necessarily stronger than the first effect, so that the cost of buying an extra unit is higher, and the size of the order is lower, resulting in a lower output.

Whether producer A will actually order $\widetilde{x}$ units and be able to sustain the order, depends on two factors: (i) are the informal units getting at least their reservation income at $\widetilde{x}$? (ii) is it in the interest of producer A to ensure that the informal units borrow from the organised market, and get their reservation income?

Let x' be the size of the order at which the informal units are just ensured of their reserve income. That is at x',

$$\pi_i = (1 + r^{**}) \, [C'(x') - C(x') \, / \, x'] \, x' = W_r$$

Two alternative configurations are possible. First, consider the case when $r^{**} > r_i^m$, i.e. the rate of interest at which the informal units can borrow from the organized credit market is higher than the rate at which they were getting loans from the formal sector. In this case the informal units will prefer to borrow from the formal sector producer, since the latter is cheaper. They will try to borrow from the organized sector only when the credit from the formal sector is no longer available. The formal sector producer A can make the organized sector's loans ineffective by simply offering the old contract.

The second possibility is $r^{**} < r_i^m$. Then, the informal units will go in for organized credit. When the informal units borrow from the organized credit market, producer A's profit-maximizing output changes to x. It has already been proved that this profit maximizing demand is lower compared to the level he was ordering when informal units did not have access to an alternative credit source, $(\tilde{x} \leq \bar{x}_m)$.

However producer A's profit may fall or increase. His loss of control over the informal producers tends to reduce his profit. On the other hand, a lower interest rate and hence a lower interest cost generates a surplus. Producer A also has the option of switching back to the old contract as long as $r^{**} > r_m$. He will choose that alternative which yields him the highest profit. Under the old contract his profit was $\prod_m^A (x_m^A)$. In the altered state, if the informal units borrow from the organized credit market, his profit will be $\prod_A(\bar{n}x)$. If $\prod_m^A (x_m^A) > \prod_A(n\tilde{x})$, he will only have to keep the old contract open to make the organized sector loan ineffective. If however he finds $\prod_m^A (x_m^A) < \prod_A(n\tilde{x})$, he would find it profitable to order $\tilde{x}$, in which case he can always withdraw his loan and ask the informal units to borrow from the organized credit market.

While choosing his profit-maximizing option, producer A's sole constraint is that the informal units will have to be guaranteed of their reservation income. If by producing $\tilde{x}$ they get less than their reservation incomes, x will never get produced. That will be the case if $\tilde{x} < x'$. Producer A will have to order x', which just guarantees the reservation income to the informal units. Alternatively, he can switch back to the old contract. Again, his choice would depend on which contract yields him a higher profit. He will order x' only if $\prod^A_m (X^A_m) \leq \prod_m (x'\bar{n})$. Otherwise he can simply keep the old contract open to draw the informal sector units away from organized sector loans.

With $r^{**} > r_m$, the informal units get a higher price in the former situation compared to the latter. For the same level of x this results in a higher income as well. So the size of the order that gives W_r to the informal units at rate of interest r^{**} will be lower compared to the same at the rate of interest r^m. $(x' \leq x_m)$. If the formal sector chooses to keep the old contract open, the organized sector's loan will be ineffective right away, and the level of output will be changed. If the loan is used, either $\tilde{x}$ or x' will be ordered. Whatever be the size of order, the output will fall.

When $r^{**} \leq r_m$, $x' \geq \bar{x}_m > \tilde{x}$. It can be shown that $\prod^A_m (x_m) \leq \prod_A (nx')$ in this situation. If the equality holds, producer A will be indifferent about choosing between the two alternatives. Otherwise he will order x'. But the point to note is that the informal producers will be confined to their reservation incomes.

So except when $\tilde{x} > x'$ and x is ordered, the lot of the informal sector units does not improve, while producer A's profit either increases or remains unchanged in all the situations considered. Whether $\tilde{x}$ will be produced at all depends on whether the formal sector finds it profitable or not. Also, the subsidy would have been more productive if it was provided to the formal sector producer directly. The output would have expanded to $\bar{x}_m$ (See Fig.6.1).

6.4   Effect of Subsidized Credit on a Variable Number of Informal Units

So far, we have assumed n to be given from outside. In this section we will consider the case when n is endogenously determined. All the other assumptions of Section 6.1 are retained.

Given n and r^*, we get a solution for x from equation (6.7). Using the implicit function theorem, this solution can be written as :

$$x_m = x_m(n, r^*);$$
$$x^m_A = x_m(n, r^*) \cdot n; \ dx_m / dn < 0 \ ; \ x_m = x_m(\bar{n}, r^*) \quad (6.9)$$

If n goes up, from equation (6.7) we can see that it increases the total output given the size of the order x_m, thereby reducing marginal revenue. So, $MR < MC$. At the optimum level x_m will have to go down to restore equality. As the number of subcontractors increase, the optimal order going to each individual subcontractor goes down.

The optimal profit function can be written as a function of n alone:

$$\prod{}^*_A = P(nx_m(n)). \; x_m(n)n - (1 + r^*) nC(x_m(n)) - nW_r$$

By maximizing the optimal profit function $w.r.t.n$, the optimal size of n is obtained. The condition that gives the optimal value of n is:

$$x(n) [P \, nx_m(n) + nx_m(n)P' \, nx_m(n)]$$

$$= (1 + r^*)C(x_m(n)) + W_r \tag{6.10}$$

The left-hand side of the equation gives the addition to revenue as each additional subcontractor is employed, and the right-hand side gives the corresponding increase in cost. The condition implies that the optimal choice of n means that the size of the order to each subcontractor is such that the parent firm's cost per subcontractor is at its minimum.

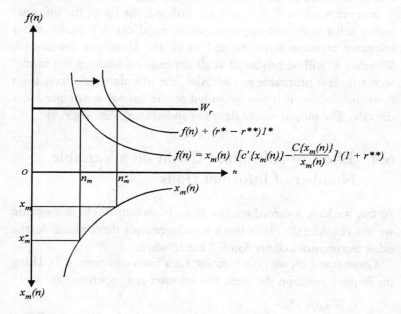

Fig. 6.2

Substituting for marginal revenue from equation (6.7) gives the condition:

$$x_m(n) \, [C' \, (x_m(n)) - C \, (x_m(n)) \, / \, x_m(n)] \, (1 + r^*) = W_r \qquad (6.10)'$$

Assuming the existence of optimal solution,[5] the optimum solution vector is (n_m, x_m). The solution is shown in Figure 6.2.

A few comments are in order here. First, in Section 6.1, we have assumed n to be given at $\bar{n}$, because producer A is in contact with $\bar{n}$ persons only. This assumption will hold true only when at $n = \bar{n}$, $d\prod_A^* / dn \geq 0$. Otherwise, producer A can always reduce n. So $\bar{n} \leq n_m$. It also follows, that the profit of producer A is higher in the equilibrium configuration (n_m, x_m) coming from free maximization of profits, compared to the equilibrium configuration $(\bar{n}, \bar{x}_m, \bar{P}_m)$ obtained from constrained maximization of profits.

Secondly, when $n = n_m$, $r_m = r^*$. For $n < n_m$, $x_m(n) > x_m(n_m)$, so, $r_i < r^*$. When the number of informal units is less than the optimum, at the rate of interest they earn more than W_r. So by proportionally reducing P_i, $1 + r_i$ below $1 + r^*$ producer A takes away this surplus. The optimum n is exactly that value of n which ensures W_r income to each individual informal unit at the rate of interest r^*.

Producer A faces two problems when he can choose n. He will have to ensure that each of the subcontractors produce $x_m \, (n_m)$, and, that they get their reservation income W_r. First, he will have to offer a higher $(1+r_i)$ to reduce output, without changing P_i correspondingly. But this reduces π_i below W_r. Then he can proportionally increase $(P_i, \, 1 + r_i)$ to increase π_i to W_r. $(1 + r_i)$ then goes up more than proportionally, causing $P_i / \, (1 + r_i)$ to go down.
Total output $n_m x_m$ will also be higher than $\bar{n} x_m$. This result follows from proposition 6.3.

Proposition 6.3: $n x_m(n)$ is an increasing function of n, for all relevant values of n.

Proof: $P \, [n x_m(n)] + n x_m(n) \, P' \, [n x_m(n)] = (1 + r^*) \, C' \, [x_m(n)]$ for all relevant values of n. Let us take $n = n_1 < n_m$, then,

$$P \, [n_1 x_m(n_1)] + n_1 x_m \, P' \, [n_1 x_m \, (n_1)] = (1 + r^*) \, C \, [x_m(n_1)]$$

Take $n_2 > n_1$, and, x_2 such that, $n_2 \, x_2 = n_1 x_m \, (n_1)$. As, $n_2 > n_1$, $x_2 < x_m(n_1)$
Then,

$$P \, [n_2 x_2] + n_2 x_2 P' \, [n_2 x_2] = n_1 x_m(n_1) P' [n_1 x_m(n_1)] + P \, [n_1 x_m(n_1)]$$

$$= (1 + r^*) \, C' \, [x_m(n_1)]$$

But, as $x_2 < x_m(n_1)$, $(1 + r^*) \, C'(x_2) < (1 + r^*) \, C' \, [x_m \, (n_1)]$.

So, $P [n_2x_2] + n_2x_2 P' [n_2x_2] > (1 + r^*) C' (x_2)$

Thus, if at $x_m(n_2)$, $P[n_2x_m(n_2)] + n_2x_m (n_2)P' [n_2x_m(n_2)] = (1 + r^*)C'$ $[x_m(n_2)] > x_2$, that is $n_1x_m(n_1) = n_2x_2 < n_2x_m(n_2)$. This implies $nx_m(n)$ is an increasing function in n.

The solution (n_m , x_m) is now compared with the solution that emerges if the informal units are allowed to borrow from the organized credit market at a rate of interest $r^{**} < r^*$. There is no loan constraint operating for the informal units either. Producer A can no longer control the rate of interest, but he can choose n. So, all the benefits of a lower rate of interest pass into the hands of producer A. The profit function for the informal unit is the same as in equation (6.1) and, their supply function is given by equation (6.2). Condition (6.3) will also hold. The problem facing the formal sector unit is:

Maximize $\prod_A = P (nx) nx - (1 + r^{**}) nC (x) - nWr n, x$

(n, x) is solved from the following conditions:

$$MR_A(n, x) = (1 + r^{**})C'(x) \qquad (6.11)$$

$$xMR_A(n, x) = (1 + r^{**})C (x) + W_r \qquad (6.12)$$

Let the solution be $(\hat{n}_m, \hat{x}_m)$. At (n_m , x_m), $\delta II_A / \delta n > 0$, $\delta II_A/\delta x > 0$. So, $\hat{n}_m > n_m, \hat{x}_m > x_m$. Also, at (n_m, x_m), $(1 + r^*) [C' (x_m) - C (x_m) / x_m]x_m = W_r$. That is at (n_m , x_m), the informal units are just guaranteed of their reservation income at the rate of interest r^{**}. Profit of A at $\hat{n}_m, \hat{x}_m$ is also higher compared to (n_m, x_m).

So provision of subsidized credit to the informal sector units here becomes equivalent to giving subsidized loans to the formal sector producer. The individual informal sector units do not gain any benefit out of the loans. Their incomes stay restricted to W_r . The parent firm extracts all the surpluses that could have accrued to the informal producing units.

6.5 Effect of Credit Constraint

In this section, we will consider the case where the formal sector producer A faces a credit constraint imposed by the organised credit market. He cannot borrow more than $\overline{L}$ amount of loan from the organized credit market. In the analysis n is treated as a variable.

As in section 6.1, initially, producer A is assumed to be the only source of credit to the informal units. The credit constraint $\overline{L}$ will only be effective if $n_mC (x_m) > \overline{L}$.

The profit function facing the informal units will be given by equation (6.1), and, their supply function by eqn. (6.2). Using proposition 6.1, and condition (6.5), it can be shown that condition (6.6) will hold.

Since, the optimal order given to each subcontractor will be the same, the informal units being identical in every respect, the problem facing producer A will be:

$$\text{Maximize } \Pi^m_A = P(nx)nx - (1 + r^*)nC(x) - nWr$$

Such that $nC(x) \leq \bar{L}$

Proposition 6.4: At $(\bar{n}, \bar{x})$, $\bar{n}C(\bar{x}) = \bar{L}$ if $(\bar{n}, \bar{x})$ is to be the optimal solution.

Proof: Suppose not. Then, $\bar{n}C(\bar{x})(\bar{x}) < \bar{L} < n_m C(x_m)$. For $\bar{n}C(\bar{x}) < \bar{L}$, producer A's profit function is $\Pi^m_A = P(nx)nx - nC(x) - nWr$, with $\delta \Pi^m / \delta n \geq 0$ for $n \leq n_m, \delta \Pi^m_A / \delta n \leq 0$ for $n_m \geq n_m, \delta \Pi^m_A / \delta x \geq$ for $x \leq x_m$. Then there will always exist some (n_a, x_a) s.t. $n_a C(x_a) = \bar{L}$, and $\Pi^m_A(n_a, x_a) > \Pi^m_A(\bar{n}, \bar{x})$. Hence, there is a contradiction. So $\bar{n}C(\bar{x}) = \bar{L}$. The maximization problem then takes the form:

$$\text{Maximize } Z = P(nx)nx - (1 + r^*) nC(x) - nW_r - \lambda[nC(x) - \bar{L}] \, x, n,$$

where λ: the lagrangian multiplier.

The solution to this problem yields the following conditions :

$$MR_A(n, x) = (1 + r^* + \lambda)C'(x) \tag{6.1}$$

$$xMR_A(n, x) = (1 + r^* + \lambda)C(x) + W_r \tag{6.2}$$

$$nC(x) = L \tag{6.3}$$

Let the solution to the system be given by $(\bar{n}, \bar{x}, \bar{\lambda})$, and assume that the solution exists and is unique for comparable values of $\bar{n}, x(n) < x_m$ (n) from equation (6.1). However, the effect of a loan constant on n is not so obvious. It is proved in proposition 6.5 that $\bar{n} < n_m$, and $\bar{x}(n) < x_m(n_m)$.

Proposition 6.5: $\bar{n} < n_m$, where n is the optimal solution in the constraint case.

Proof: Suppose not. Then $\bar{n} > n_m$.

Uniqueness of (n_m, x_m) and $(\bar{n}, \bar{x})$ rules out $n = n_m$, so, $\bar{n} > n_m$.

From equation (2c) $\bar{n}C(\bar{x}) = \bar{L}$. So, $n_m C(\bar{x}) < \bar{L} < n_m C(x_m)$. Then, $\exists$ some $x_k > \bar{x}$ for which $n_m C(x_k) = \bar{L}$. This implies (n_m, x_m) belongs to the feasible set of solutions. Also, $x_k < x_m$. Now, $\delta \Pi^m_A / \delta x \geq 0$ for $x \leq x_m$, and, $\delta \Pi^m_A / \delta n \leq$ for $n \geq n_m$, that is, $\Pi^m_A(\bar{n}, \bar{x}) < \Pi^m_A(n_m, x_k)$.

Then $(\bar{n}, \bar{x})$ cannot be optimum. Hence, $\bar{n}$ cannot be greater than n_m. So we conclude $\bar{n} < n_m$.

Proposition 6.6: $\bar{x}(\bar{n}) < x_m(n_m)$.

Proof: Suppose not, then $\bar{x}(\bar{n}) < x_m(n_m)$. This implies $(1 + r^* + \lambda)$ $[C'(\bar{x}) / \bar{x}] > (1 + r^*) [C'(x_m) - C(x_m)/x_m]x_m = W_r$. But this violates condition (6.2). So, $\bar{x}(\bar{n}) < x_m(n_m)$.

As is expected, both the size of the order and the number of subcontractors employed are reduced compared to (n_m, x_m). It follows that the total output will go down along with the profit of the formal sector producer A.

Here $(1 + r_i) = (1 + r^* + \lambda) = MR_A \cdot \lambda C'(x)$, which implies $P_i = MR_A$

In this framework, let us check how the results get altered if the informal units are allowed to borrow from the organized credit market directly, at an interest rate $r^{**} \leq r^*$. If there is no credit constraint for the informal units, then, producer A will operate exactly as in section 6.4. He would choose $\hat{x}_m > x_m > \bar{x}$, and, $\hat{n}_m > n_m > \bar{n}$. The profit of the informal units exactly guarantees them their reservation incomes. Total output will increase. The effect of providing subsidized loans to the informal units is equivalent in effect to giving the same amount of subsidized credit to the formal sector producer. Producer A completely substitutes his high cost loan by the low cost loan available to the informal units and, also circumvents the credit rationing he faces in the organized credit market. The informal units do not benefit from the subsidized loans, all the benefits accrue to producer A.

If the individual informal units face a loan constraint of amount l^*, the constraint will only be operative if $C(x_m) > l^*$. Then, part of the funds has to be provided by producer A. In other words, he cannot completely substitute the more expensive loan by the cheaper loan. He can operate either as a primary lender or as a residual lender. But if he acts as a primary lender, he will have to give loans at $r \leq r^{**} \leq r^*$. If $r^{**} = r^*$, he will be indifferent. If however, $r^{**} < r^*$, then he will have to incur a loss. Also, it will be profitable for him to encourage the informal units to exhaust cheaper loans first. We will only consider the case where producer A acts as a residual lender, since for $r^{**} = r^*$, the two cases will yield the same result. The effective rate of interest facing the informal units will be:

$$r' = r [C(x) - l^*] / C(x) + r^{**} [l^*/C(x) \quad \text{for } C(x) \geq l^* \qquad (6.4)$$

(The subscripts have been dropped for convenience since it makes no difference.)

The profit function facing the informal unit will be given by:

$$\pi = px - (1 + r)\,[C(x) - l^*] - (1 + r^{**})l^* \tag{6.5}$$

The supply function will be the same as in eqn.(6.2) The formal sector's profit function is:

$$\prod{}''_A = P(nx)nx - (1 + r^*)nC(x) - n\,[px - (1 + r)$$
$$\{c(x) - l^*\} - (1 + r^{**})l] \tag{6.6}$$

Proposition 6.1 will hold good here, also. So that if $\pi = W_r$. then, the profit function for the formal sector reduces to :

$$\prod{}''_A = P\,(nx)nx - (1 + r^*)\,nC(x) + nl^*(r^* - r^{**}) - nW_r. \tag{6.6}$$

The profit maximizing choice of (n, x) is obtained from the following two conditions:

$$MR_A(n, x) = (1 + r^*)C'\,(x) \tag{6.7}$$

$$xMR_A(n, x) = (1 + r^*)C\,(x) + W_r - (r^* - r^{**})\,l^*. \tag{6.8}$$

Let the solution be (x''_m, n''_m). For $r^{**} = r^*$, the solution will coincide with (x_m, n_m). If $r^{**} < r^*$, then there is an additional gain when each additional subcontractor is employed as it enables producer A to substitute l^* units of a dearer loan by the same amount of a cheaper loan. Producer A will find it in his interest to employ a greater number of subcontractors than n_m. Since the marginal cost is the same as in section 6.2, increasing n beyond n_m would imply $MR_A(n''_m, x_m) < (1 + r^*)\,C'(x_m)$. This is because, given the marginal cost, increase in n beyond n_m, with x unchanged at x_m implies expanding the total output beyond the profit maximizing level. To maintain the output at the profit maximizing level, x must go down. Thus $\overline{x} < x''_m < x_m$. In terms of Fig. 6.2 the curve $f(n)$ has a parallel shift to $f(n) + (r^* - r^{**})l^*$. So, n increases beyond n_m, implying a fall in $x_m(n)$.

Here, the rate of interest at which producer A lends to the informal units will coincide with r^*. The reason is the same as given earlier. Also the effect of providing each of the n''_m informal units l^* amount of loans at the rate of interest r^{**}, is equivalent in effect to that of providing the formal sector producer with $n''_m l^*$ amount of additional loans over and above $\overline{L}$ at the subsidized interest rate r^{**}, making the availability of additional loans dependent upon the number of subcontractors employed.

This solution can only be realized when $n''_m C(x''_m) - n''_m l^*. \leq \overline{L}$. However, if $n''_m C(x''_m) - n''_m\, l^* > \overline{L}$ then, the formal sector's loan constraint will not allow him to give an order x''_m, to each of the n''_m subcontractors, because he cannot provide the excess fund required to support that particular order. Then, the formal sector producer will choose that (n, x) for which the total fund $\bar{L} + nl^*$ gets exhausted. Again, as the informal units are borrowing from two sources, their effective rate of interest will be given by equation (6.4), and, their profit function will be the same as equation (6.5). Following identical arguments, producer A's profit function will be given by equation (6.6). But the problem for producer A now becomes:

Maximize $\prod''_A$ s.t.$nC(x) - nl^* = \bar{L}$ which is equivalent to maximizing:

$$Z = P(nx)nx - (1 + r^*)nC(x) - nW_r + (r^* - r^{**})nl^* - \gamma[nC(x) - nl^* - \bar{L}]$$

where, γ: is the lagrangian multiplier.

Optimum levels of (n, x) are obtained from the conditions:

$$MR_A(n, x) = (1 + r^* + \gamma)C'(x) \tag{6.6}$$

$$xMR_A(n, x) = (1 + r^* + \gamma)C(x) + W_r - (r^* - r^{**})t^* - \gamma l^* \tag{6.7}$$

$$nC(x) - nl^* = \bar{L}. \tag{6.8}$$

Let the solution be ($\bar{\bar{n}}$, $\bar{\bar{x}}$).

The loans given to the informal units have the effect of alleviating the loan constraint faced by producer A. Consider the case $r^* = r^{**}$, i.e. no subsidy is given to the informal units. Then it is obvious that (n, x) will increase as additional loans of amount nl^* becomes available, and the loan constraint is relaxed.

For $r^{**} < r^*$, there is an additional advantage of substituting the more expensive loans by the cheaper loan. The relevant profit function is $\prod''_A$ not $\prod'''_A$. As a result, n increases by more and x increases by less compared to the situation $r^{**} = r^*$. But, as, at $(\bar{n}, \bar{x})$ $nC(x) - nl^*$ $< \bar{L}$ and $\delta\prod''A / \delta n > 0$, $\delta\prod''A / \delta x > 0$, at (n, x) $\bar{\bar{n}} > \bar{n}$, $\bar{\bar{x}} > \bar{x}$ will still hold. Here also the loans provided to the informal units produce the same effect they would have produced, if they were provided to the formal sector producer A, conditional upon employing additional subcontractors.

6.6 Conclusion

The above analysis suggests that, providing subsidized credit directly to the individual informal units may not be conducive to the welfare of the individual units. The linkage between the formal sector units and the informal sector units plays a very important role in determining the effect of a specific policy. Also, the informal units may face constraints on more than one front. So, rather than implementing a generalized policy in order to promote the small informal units, it would be better to make a detailed study of the informal sector and use situation specific policies. It is also true, that often the growth of the formal industrial sector and the informal sector are linked together. For example, in this paper, growth in the profit and output of the formal sector has resulted in an increase in the number of subcontractors employed. In such situations policies that promote the organized industrial sector (formal sector) would be an improvement.

Notes

1. This is a simplifying assumption; we can substitute an oligopolistic or competitive structure, and, with quite simple assumptions the same results will be obtained.
2. This assumption can be justified by arguing that, to produce x, the formal sector producer has to incur a huge cost. There are certain rigidities within the system, which do not allow a reduction in costs even when output falls, whereas, no substantial economies of scale are gained by large scale production.
3. Here, sales costs are ignored because their inclusion will not affect the analysis in any way, as the costs will be there in all the cases considered.
4. The formal proof of this proposition can be found in Gangopadhyay and Sengupta (1987).
5. The assumptions about the nature of the demand and cost function guarantees about the second order condition for profit maximization is satisfied in all the cases considered.

References

Bardhan, P.K. (1980). Interlocking Factor Markets and Agrarian Developments: A Review of Issues. *Oxford Economic Papers* 32: 82–98.

Basu, K. (1983). The Emergence of Isolation and Interlinkage in Rural Markets. *Oxford Economic Papers* 35: 262–280.

(1984). *The Less Developed Economy: A Critique of Contemporary Theory*. Oxford: Basil Blackwell.

(1986). One Kind of Power. *Oxford Economic Papers* 38: 259–282.

Basu, T. (1977). Calcutta's Sandal Makers. *Economic and Political Weekly* August 6, Vol. 12.

(1977). Hosiery Workers of Calcutta. *Economic and Political Weekly* December 17, Vol. 12.

Bose, A.N. (1978). *Calcutta and Rural Bengal: Small Sector Symbiosis.* Calcutta: Minerva Associates Publications P.Ltd.

S. Gangopadhyay, S. and K. Sengupta. (1987). Small Farmers, Moneylenders and Trading Activity. *Oxford Economic Papers* 12: 1–40.

Harris, J. (1982). Character of an Urban Economy: Small Scale Production and Labour Markets in Coimbatore. *Economic and Political Weekly* 17, 23 and 24: 954, 993–1001.

Nagraj, R. (1984). Subcontracting in Indian Manufacturing Industries. *Economic and Political Weekly* 19, 31–33 (Annual Number): 1435–1463.

Oi, W. (1971). A Disneyland Dilemma: Two-part Tariffs for a Mickey Mouse Monopoly. *Quarterly Journal of Economics* 85: 77–96.

Romatate, E. (1983). Calcutta's Informal Sector: Theory and Reality. *Economic and Political Weekly* 17, 15: 2115–2128.

Roy, D. and K. Sengupta. (1989). Interlinkages and Pattern of Competition. In *The Economic Theory of Agrarian Institutions*, ed. P.K. Bardhan. Oxford: Clarendon Press.

Watanabe, S. (1971). Subcontracting, Industrialization, and Employment Creation. *International Labour Review* 6, 1–2: 51–76.

Strategic Aspects of Overseas Equity Joint Ventures

Sugata Marjit

7.1 Introduction

Joint ventures, as organizational forms of direct foreign investment have drawn considerable attention in recent years. This has been particularly evident in the context of the Chinese economy, where the number of investment projects featuring partial to complete equity-control by foreigners have increased significantly in recent years.[1] While some countries have demonstrated a greater degree of openness towards foreign investors, quite a few of the developing countries are still skeptical about allowing operational freedom to the multinationals. Restriction on equity participation by foreigners has led to alternative ways of market penetration such as technology licensing, marketing contracts, subsidiary formations, etc. A case in point is that of India.[2] Until recently, foreign equity participation in Indian business was quite restricted.

The form of overseas investment or the multinationals' strategies for gaining entry into foreign markets are conditioned by various factors, economic and political. In some cases a foreign firm might be interested in the direct export of a product rather than in direct foreign investment (DFI) or in technology licensing.[3] There is an inherent commitment problem in the very nature of DFI. Investment is usually like a 'sunk' cost and several types of risk attend the appropriation of benefits flowing from investment. The 'expropriation' or 'hostage' problem is quite well known in economics. One way of binding the host government to its commitment to 'protect' foreign investment is through a scheme whereby the local government shares some part of the financial burden. A model of this form has been attempted in Marjit (1990) which has been recently extended to include 'reputational' considerations allowing for sequential entry by a large number of multinationals in Mitra and Marjit (1992). The main idea in these papers is that the foreign firms might 'like' host capital participation as an 'insurance' against harmful future actions by local political authorities. Following this line of research in Section 7.2 of this paper, we develop a framework where equity joint ventures help to 'signal' the good intention of the local government. In particular, the efficient equity-sharing schemes depend on the asymmetric risk perception of the foreign firm and the host government regarding the investment project.[4]

Another important motivation of the paper comes from the hypothesis that the foreign firms might sometimes like to control as much equity as possible to ensure corporate control. While transferring technology to a local firm a multinational might be quite concerned about: a) the imitation and subsequent piracy of the knowledge particularly when intellectual property rights are hard to enforce across national boundaries; b) actions on the part of the local subsidiary which might hurt the 'brand-name' reputation; c) being unable to practice 'transfer-pricing', which is possible through full-scale integration, etc. Such concerns might lead to a sub-optimal technology transfer in a pure technology agreement. These problems have been discussed in relation to the Indian economy (Singh 1992; UNCTAD 1983). In the present context allowing some degree of equity control to the foreign firm helps to improve the situation. In Section 7.3 we attempt a simple analysis by integrating the issue of technology transfer with equity joint venture.

This paper tries to show that the sharing of investments along with the profits helps in implementing relatively efficient equilibria in an otherwise distorted world. In some cases the foreign firms like to invest as 'little' capital as possible and in some others they might like to run the business on their own. This is elaborated and summed up in the last section.

7.2   Differential Risk and Equity Joint Venture

Consider a situation where a firm is contemplating investment in a foreign country today and expecting the pay-off tomorrow. There are two types of risk associated with such a project. First, the project-specific risk, i.e. uncertainty about factors affecting the demand for the product to be produced, production conditions, availability of required inputs, etc. Second, the country specific risk which is primarily due to the government deviating from some 'announced' policies. Both of these risks are summarized by a probability p of success and $(1 - p)$ of failure.

Let $R(I)$ be the concave profit-function gross of investment cost I. If r is the rate of discount, then the firm maximizes,

$$\underset{I}{Max} \left[p.\frac{R(I)}{1+r} + (1-p) \frac{0}{1+r} - I \right] \tag{7.1}$$

which yields

$$\frac{R'(I)}{1+r} = \frac{1}{p} \tag{7.2}$$

Let $I = I_p$ solve eqn. (7.2)

Hence, the firm gets,

$$\pi (I_p) = p \frac{R(I_p)}{1+r} - I_p \tag{7.3}$$

The benefit function faced by the host government is assumed to be in I.

$$\pi_g = \alpha, I \text{ where } \alpha > 0 \tag{7.4}$$

Eqn. (7.4) is justified by the fact that a greater volume of investment helps to employ more people in an economy with a significant rate of unemployment and therefore directly leads to greater social welfare. Many developing countries suffer from acute foreign exchange crisis. Higher investments in terms of foreign exchange help such an ailing economy.

Therefore, the benefit accruing to the local government is,

$$\pi g\,(I_p) = \alpha,\,I_p \tag{7.5}$$

While summarizing the risk elements in terms of p, we have mentioned country-specific risk, which mainly arises due to uncertain government actions. In this case we assume that the government has the required political will to commit to the 'announced' policies. If the government could run the investment project on its own, it would probably face the same project-specific risk. However, the political risk factor would be absent in that case. This would have entailed a success probability $q > p$ for the project. Although the government is committed to its policies it is very hard to signal its commitment to the multinational, which perceives the success probability to be lower than q.

Since $q > p$, $I_q > I_p$. This follows from eqn. (7.2) and the concavity of $R(I)$. As the benefit function is linear in I, the local government loses the difference between I_q and I_p. A straightforward way of achieving Iq is through subsidizing a part of the investment. This raises the problem of financing subsidies. If the benefits from such a project are not 'tangible', it cannot be self-financed. However, an equity sharing scheme, by which the government shares investment against a share in the profits, could be designed so as to increase the level of investment. We call this an equity joint venture[5] (EJV). The investment decision continues to rest with the firm. We also assume that this is a binding contract. We now prove that such a scheme exists, noting that the alternative scheme is one wherein the multinational guarantees a return of $\pi\,(I_p)$.

In an EJV contract the foreign firm shares θ_1 fraction of revenue against a θ_2 share in investment.

A feasible EJV contract is defined by $c(\theta_1, \theta_2)$, satisfying

$$q\,\frac{R(I)}{1+r}\,-I-\left[\theta_1 p\frac{R(I)}{1+r}\,-\,\theta_2 I\right] \geq 0 \tag{7.6}$$

$$\theta_1 p\,\frac{R(I)}{1+r}\,-\,\theta_2 I \;\geq\; \pi\,(I_p) \tag{7.7}$$

$$I > I_p \tag{7.8}$$

$$0 < \theta_1,\, < 1,\;\; 0 < \theta_2 < 1 \tag{7.9}$$

In offering such a contract, the local government believes that the project will yield, for any investment I,

$$q \frac{R(I)}{1+r} - I$$

However, the multinational believes that the project should earn $p R(I)/1 + r$ for any I and is consequently concerned about eqn. (7.7). We are interested in (θ_1, θ_2) satisfying the constraints (7.6) – (7.9). Note that the constrained 'first-best' in the model is given by I_q, which solves

$$\frac{R'(I_q)}{1+r} = \frac{1}{q} \tag{7.10}$$

and generates $\pi (I_q)$. We now prove the following proposition.

Proposition 1:   There exists $C(\theta_1, \theta_2)$ satisfying (7.6) – (7.9) and implementing Iq.

Proof: Consider $\theta_2 = p/q \; \theta_1$. Since the foreign firm maximizes $(\theta_1 p R(I) / 1 + r - \theta_2 I)$, it must choose $I = I_q$, i.e. $\theta_2 = p / q \; \theta_1$. Substituting for θ_1 in (7.7) with strict equality we get, $\theta_2 = \pi (I_p) / \pi(I_q) < 1$ as $I_q > I_p$. If eqn. (7.7) holds with strict equality and $I = I_q$, (7.6) is satisfied with strict inequality as $\pi (I_q) > \pi (I_p)$.

We have to check whether for $\theta_2 = \dfrac{\pi (I_p)}{\pi (I_q)}, \; \theta_1 < 1.$

Now, $\theta_1 = \dfrac{q}{p} . \dfrac{\pi (I_p)}{\pi (I_q)} = \dfrac{\dfrac{\pi (I_q)}{p}}{\Big/ \dfrac{\pi (I_q)}{q}}$

$\theta_1 < 1 \Rightarrow \dfrac{\pi (I_p)}{p} < \dfrac{\pi (I_q)}{q}$. As $q > p$, we have to prove that

$$\frac{d \left[\dfrac{\pi(I_p)}{p} \right]}{dp} > 0$$

$$\frac{\pi(I_p)}{p} = \frac{\dfrac{pR(I_p)}{1+r} - I_p}{p}$$

$$\frac{d\left(\dfrac{\pi(I_p)}{p}\right)}{dp} = \frac{p\left[\dfrac{\partial \pi(I_p)}{\partial I_p} \cdot \dfrac{dI_p}{dp} + \dfrac{R(I_p)}{1+r}\right] - \pi(I_p)}{p^2}$$

$$= \frac{\dfrac{pR(I_p)}{1+r} - \pi(I_p)}{p^2} > 0 \text{ by}$$

using the condition that $\dfrac{\partial \pi(I_p)}{\partial p} = 0$.

Hence, $\dfrac{\pi(I_p)}{p}$ increases with p. Therefore, $\theta_1 < 1$. QED

We have assumed that an EJV contract does not alter the perceived risk of the project as envisaged by the foreign firm. The sharing rule is so chosen that it implements I_q. However, p might itself be affected by θ_2. When $\theta_2 = 1$, i.e., in the initial situation the firm starts with p. As θ_2 increases, p might increase. When the government finances the investment entirely, p is equal to q. One can postulate the following function,

$$p(\theta_2) = p + (q - p)(1 - \theta_2) \tag{7.11}$$

Eqn. (7.11) implies that as θ_2 is reduced from 1 to 0, $p(\theta_2)$ increases from p to q. One can extend the former proof in this context noting that $p'(\theta_2) < 0$ and $\pi(I_p)/p(\theta_2)$ is decreasing in θ_2.

To sum up, what we have shown in this section is that the local government shares in investment in a project along with the foreign firm investment. The risk factor faced by the firm can be reduced somewhat through the government's participation. One could also accommodate a situation where the foreign firm actually gains by making eqn. (7.7) not binding. Reducing θ_2 should be a welcome decision to the firm as well as the government as it helps to increase the net surplus generated in the project.[6] In the next section we discuss a set-up in a foreign firm with larger θ_2.

7.3 Technology Agreement and EJV

This theoretical exercise is based upon the Indian experience. After the Rajiv Gandhi government took over in 1984, a liberalized trade/investment policy was announced. The policy focused on removing barriers for technology and capital-goods import and not on removing tariff barriers for attracting DFI. In such a policy environment, foreign firms chose to penetrate the Indian market through technological collaborations with Indian businessmen.

We start from a situation where a local firm tries to obtain a 'new' technology from a foreign firm. The foreign firm licenses the technology at a royalty fee determined by the local political authorities. However, technologies of several generations are available to the foreign source. It decides on what to transfer. This choice is important because the foreign firm cannot be guaranteed against subsequent 'imitation' or misuse of technology.[7] Further, it might be worried about its brand-name reputation if the subsidiary is unable to maintain the quality of the licensed product/technology. Since equity-participation by a foreign firm gives a degree of corporate-control to the technology supplier, an EJV contract will raise the level of technology transferred.

To assert this basic point we take recourse to a simple analytical model. Suppose that the level of technologies available to the foreign source is represented by a set $T = \{t\}$, $t \, \varepsilon [0, \bar{t}]$, $t = 0$ represents the "worst" technology and $\bar{t}$ the "best". The profits from using t is given by $R(t)$ $R' > 0$, $R'' = 0$. The foreign firm uses $\bar{t}$ as it fetches the maximum profit. Initially there is only one local firm which has some technology level $0 < $ to $< \bar{t}$. The foreign firm is not allowed to export its product or to invest directly. The domestic firm, which is importing new technology has to set up a new unit with an investment I (independent of the level of technology). The net pay-off to the local firm after the transfer of technology t is,

$$R(t) - I - R(t_0) - P_s, \tag{7.12}$$

where P_s is the royalty it has to pay to the technology supplier. Suppose that $\lambda(R(t) - I - R(t_0))$ is the fee accruing to the foreign supplier. For $[R(t) - I - R(t_0)] > 0$ we assume that $[R(\bar{t}) - I - R(t_0)] > 0$.

The foreign firm is worried about the subsequent use of its technology. *This is true for the public-good characteristics of a technology.* As long as the domestic firm had a technology level 't_0', the foreign firm was not worried because 't_0' was not good enough to pose a threat to the firm's existing market share outside the country. However, as t rises above t_0, the potential threat of entry increases. This threat is 'perceived', even if it is not actually posed by the domestic firm. We capture this threat perception in the following function,

$$R^* = R^* (t, t_0) \qquad (7.13)$$

with $R^* (\bar{t}, t) = \overline{R}^*$ for $t < t_0$

and $R^* (\bar{t}, t) < \overline{R}^*$ for $t > t_0$

$$\frac{\partial R^*}{\partial t} < 0, \quad \frac{\partial^2 R^*}{\partial t^2} < 0$$

Eqn. 7.13 states that for $t > t_0$, the entry-threat is effective, otherwise, there will be a decline in profit through an uncontrolled subsidiary. In case the multinational is allowed equity participation in the venture, it can 'control' the operations better keeping in mind its network of business in the rest of the world. However, its control may not be so perfect as to eliminate all risks. But the probability that it can avoid some of these problems increases. We denote such a probability by $p = p(\theta)$ where θ is the share of I borne by the multinational. The expected-profit function is,

$$R^*_E = p(\theta)R^* + (1 - p(\theta))R^* (\bar{t}, t) \qquad (7.14)$$

$p' > 0$, with $p(0) = 0$, $p(1) = 1$

for $\theta = 0$

$$R^*_E = R^* (\bar{t}, t) \qquad (7.15)$$

The quality of technology to be transferred is to be decided by the foreign firm which maximizes,

$$\underset{t}{Max} \; \lambda \left[R(t) - R(t_0) - I \right] + R^* (\bar{t}, t) \qquad (7.16)$$

The First Order Condition (F.O.C)

$$R'(t) = - \frac{\partial R^*}{\partial t} \cdot \frac{1}{\lambda} \qquad (7.17)$$

The Second Order Condition (S.O.C) is satisfied as $R(t) = 0$ and $\partial^2 R^*/\partial t^2 < 0$.

Let $\tilde{t}$ solve eqn. (7.17). We also assume that $R(\tilde{t}) > R(t_0) - I$ (18).[8] The local firm receives $(1 - \lambda) [R(\tilde{t}) - R(t_0) - I]$ and the foreign firm receives $\lambda[R(\tilde{t}) - R(t_0) - I + R^* (t, \tilde{t})]$. Note that in this binding contract, the local firm promises to pay $\lambda[R(\tilde{t}) - R(t_0) - I]$ to the foreigner. While in any other contract $[R(t) - R(t_0) - I]$ would be the alternative pay-off to the foreign firm by the local authorities; the multinational also takes into account $R^*(\bar{t}, \tilde{t})$. We shall see that such an assumption can be easily dropped without altering the basic result.

Since the local firm would always like higher t, there is room for designing a proper incentive scheme so that $t > \tilde{t}$. We now construct an EJV scheme to induce the multinational to transfer a $t > \tilde{t}$ without loss to itself. Suppose that the foreign firm is allowed to share a part of I in a partnership venture earning some share of the profit. So now it has income from two sources: (1) the fee for transferred technology and, (2) the share of the net profits as a business partner. If θ_1 is the foreign firm's share in the profits and θ_2 is its share of investment, we define an EJV contract, $C(\theta_1, \theta_2)$ as a contract satisfying the following conditions:

$$R(t) - R(t_0) - I - [\lambda(R(t) - R(t_0) - I)] -$$

$$[\theta_1(R(t) - R(t_0) - \theta_2 I] \geq (1 - \lambda)\,[R(\tilde{t}) - R(t_0) - I] \qquad (7.19)$$

$$\lambda[R(t) - R(t_0) - I] +$$

$$[\theta_1(R(t) - R(t_0)) - \theta_2 I] \geq \lambda[R(\tilde{t}) - R(t_0) - I] \qquad (7.20)$$

$$\lambda[R(t) - R(t_0) - I] + (1 - p(\theta_2))\,R^*(\bar{t}, t) + p(\theta_2)\,\overline{R}^*$$

$$[\theta_1(R(t) - R(t_0)) - \theta_2 I] \geq \lambda[R(\tilde{t}) - R(t_0) - I] + R^*(\bar{t}, \tilde{t}) \quad (7.21)$$

$$0 < \theta_1 < 1, \quad 0 < \theta_2 < 1. \qquad (7.22)$$

Eqn. (7.19) is the participation constraint or the incentive constraint for the local firm. Eqn. (7.20) is the official incentive constraint for the foreign firm. Eqn. (7.21) is the true incentive constraint faced by the foreign firm. Eqn. (7.22) specifies the range of θ_1, θ_2.

We now prove the following proposition.

Proposition 2:   There exists $c(\theta_1, \theta_2)$ satisfying eqn. (7.19) – (7.22) and implementing $t > \tilde{t}$.

Proof: We start with a scheme $\theta_1 = \theta_2 = \theta$, treat eqn. (7.19) with equality and then prove that $c(\theta, \theta)$ is a possible candidate for the solution.

The foreign firm maximizes,

$$\underset{t}{Max}\ \lambda\left[R(t) - R(t_o) - I\right] + p(\theta)\,\overline{R}^* +$$

$$(1 - p(\theta))R^*(\bar{t}, t) + \theta\left[R(t) - R(t_o)\right] - \theta\,I$$

The F.O.C.

$$R'(t) = \frac{1 - p(\theta))}{\lambda + \theta} \left(-\frac{\partial R^*}{\partial t} \right) \tag{7.23}$$

(S.O.C. is satisfied).

Let $\hat{t}$ solve eqn. (7.23). Note that,

$$\hat{t} > \tilde{t} \quad as \quad \frac{1 - p(\theta)}{\lambda + \theta} - \frac{1}{\lambda} = \frac{-(\lambda p(\theta) + \theta)}{\lambda(\lambda + \theta)} < 0$$

From eqn. (7.19) (with equality)

$$\theta = (1 - \lambda) \frac{R(\hat{t}) - R(\tilde{t})}{R(\hat{t}) - R(t_o) - I} = \hat{\theta} \tag{7.24}$$

Note that $0 < \hat{\theta} < 1$, as $R(\hat{t}) - R(\tilde{t}) < R(\hat{t}) - R(t_0) - I$. Since, $\hat{t} > \tilde{t}$, (7.20) would be satisfied with strict inequality for any $0 < \theta < 1$, and hence for $\theta = \hat{\theta}$. Eqn. (7.21) is satisfied with strict inequality as $p(\theta) \bar{R}^* + (1 - p(\theta)) R^* (t, \hat{t}) > R^*(t, \tilde{t})$.

Hence, the proposition.   QED

For any $0 < \theta < \hat{\theta}$, eqn. (7.19) would hold with strict inequality. As t should be monotonically increasing in θ, $\tilde{t} < t(\theta) < \hat{t}$. Therefore, eqns. (7.20), (7.21) would continue to hold with inequality even for $t < \hat{t}$, as long as $t > \tilde{t}$. In such a situation the local firm is not necessarily pushed onto its reservation pay-off. A possible way of increasing t is through an increase in λ. But such a scheme can be implemented without altering λ and just by choosing appropriate 'θ'.

One can reformulate the incentive-problem in game-theoretic terms. For example, the government might act as a Stackelberg leader by choosing some θ (given λ) and internalizing the resulting change in t to maximize the net benefit of the local firm. Such a problem can be set up by rewriting eqn. (7.19) in the following manner:

$$(1 - \lambda) (R(t) - R(\tilde{t})) - \theta [R(t) - R(t_0) - I] \tag{7.25}$$

The problem then is to maximize eqn. (7.25) with respect to θ, where $t = t(\theta)$ from eqn. (7.23)) with $t' > 0$. It is easy to check whether such a 'θ' will satisfy eqn. (7.20) and (7.21).[9]

7.4   Conclusion

This paper attempted to provide a strategic rationale for equity joint ventures in an international context. We have discussed two cases. In the first case EJV arises as a means of pooling risk between two agents who have different perceptions about the risk associated with an investment project. We have argued why such a differential risk perception would be a natural-analytical premise in many situations involving overseas investment. In the second case we provide another example where the foreign investor would like to retain corporate control, and without equity participation, tends to transfer a sub-optimal level of technology, threatened by the negative externalities associated with the use of transferred technology.

Situations such as the first case call for greater participation of the local capital as an insuring device. Whereas the second case actually points towards the foreign ownership of a venture for the 'best' result. A natural extension of our analysis is to integrate these two aspects in a unified model and try to characterize the optimal 'θ' in that context. However, one should be aware of the importance of the special cases discussed in the paper as they tend to capture country-specific attributes in the context of a given political and historical background. It would be difficult to construct cases where all the reasons for designing an EJV scheme are present simultaneously. Therefore, a case-by-case analysis might turn out to be as important as the one with an integrated structure. When summing up one should mention that while discussing an EJV contract we have assumed that such a contract is honoured by the local participant. In a dynamic context such commitments should be analysed as "subgame perfect solutions", which we do not attempt here.

Notes

1. See the section on Chinese economy in the *Asian Development Outlook* (1992) and Campbell (1988).
2. See Bagchi (1987), Singh (1992), and the *Asian Development Outlook* (1992).
3. For entry-related strategies in a foreign market see Tang and Yu (1990). Also see Kabiraj (1993) for a recent discussion on the host government policy towards the form of foreign participation.
4. On 'Transfer Pricing' and Joint Ventures, see Katrak (1983), Falvey and Fried (1986), Gangopadhyay and Gang (1993). For an analysis of joint ventures in a different context see Sejnar and Smith (1984). See also Schweinberger (1991).
5. One can also term this as a 'tax-subsidy' scheme. For that matter in any partnership venture, partners share the investment cost against a share of the profits. When the government is one of the partners, this becomes similar to a 'tax-subsidy' scheme. In a joint venture scheme the subsidy cost is raised directly from the venture itself. Typically, subsidization by

the government may be funded by any 'other' source not specifically by the returns in the subsidized project.

6. Since the benefit accruing to the government is linear in investment, $I > Iq$ would be more profitable from the government's point of view. However, eqn. (7.6) must be satisfied under any circumstances. $\theta_1 = q / p \, \theta_2$ and eqn. (7.7) give us *one* of the possible sharing rules. In fact $\theta_1 > q / p \, \theta_2$, could still do it by making $I > I_q$. But one must then take into account that $qR(I) / 1 + r \doteq I < q \, R(I_q) / 1 + r - I_q$. Our purpose has not been to characterize an optimal EJV contract but to indicate the feasibility of an EJV contract.

7. See Kabiraj and Marjit (1992, 1993).

8. For the existence of a $\widetilde{t}$, it seems we are making an awful lot of assumptions. We do it just to focus on the issue of EJV and technology transfer. A detailed and rigorous analysis on the quality of transferred technology in a Cournot-Nash framework is provided in Kabiraj and Marjit (1993). Here the main point is not to focus on the technology transfer equilibrium *per se* but to see how such an equilibrium is affected through an EJV contract.

9. One needs two additional conditions here for the existence of a meaningful 'θ'. (a) $1 - \lambda > \theta$, (b) $d^2 t / d \theta^2 < 0$.

Note that when the local firm is pushed to its reservation pay-off $\theta = \hat{\theta} \, 1 - \lambda$. In the Stackelberg solution it is likely that $\theta < \hat{\theta}$ as the net pay-off to the local firm is decreasing in θ. In that case θ should be less than $1 - \lambda$. Condition (b) is more technical in nature. Also note that in case the local government knows about eqn. (7.21), then eqn. (7.20) becomes irrelevant and that does not alter our analysis.

References

Asian Development Outlook. (1992). Published by the Asian Development Bank (ADB).

Bagchi, A.K. (1987). *Public Intervention and Industrial Restructuring in South Korea, India and China*. ILO Publication ARTEP.

Campbell, N. (1988). *The Patterns of Equity Joint Ventures in China*. Manchester Business School, Working Paper No.156.

Falvey R. and H. Fried. (1986). National ownership requirements and transfer pricing. *Journal of Development Economics* 24: 249–254.

Gangopadhyay, S. and I. Gang. (1993). *Foreign direct vs. foreign indirect investment: The issue of control and optimal government policy*. Rutgers University, Working Paper No.21.

Kabiraj, T. and S. Marjit. (1992). To Transfer or not to Transfer the Best Technology under Potential Threat of Entry – The Case of Price Competition. In *Game Theory and Economic Applications*, ed. T. Parthasarathi et al. Springer-Verlag.

(1993). International Technology Transfer under Potential Threat of Entry – A Cournot-Nash Framework. *Journal of Development Economics* 42: 75–88.

Kabiraj, T. (1993). Tariff vs. Licensing in the Presence of Fixed Costs. *Journal of International Trade and Economic Development* 2: 27–41.

Katrak, H. (1983). Multinational firm's global strategies, host country indigenisation of ownership and welfare. *Journal of Development Economics* 31: 331–348.

Marjit, S. (1990). Rationalizing Public-Private Joint Ventures in an Open Economy – A Strategic Approach. *Journal of Development Economics* 33: 377–383.

Moitra, B. and S. Marjit. (1992). Multinational Entry, Expropriation and Contract Compliance under a Boycott Threat. University of Rochester, Working Paper No.307.

Schweinberger, A. (1991). *Joint Ventures in Mixed Economies*, (mimeo). University of Konstanz.

Singh, N. (1992). Multinationals, Technology and Government Policy. In *Development Policy and Economic Theory*, ed. K. Basu and P. Nayak. Delhi: Oxford University Press.

Sejnar, J. and S.C. Smith. (1984). The economies of joint ventures in less developed countries. *Quarterly Journal of Economics* 119: 149–167.

Tang, M. and C. Yu. (1990). Foreign Market Entry: Product Related Strategies. *Management Science* 36: 476–89.

UNCTAD. (1983). *Technology Issues in the Capital Goods Sector: A Case Study of Leading Machinery Producers in India*. Geneva.

The Effects of Creating Free Trade Zones in the Presence of a Binding Foreign Exchange Constraint

Smita Adhikary
and
Tamal Datta Chaudhuri*

8.1 Introduction

The literature[1] on free trade zones (FTZs) has concentrated primarily on the second best properties of creating such zones. That is, in the

* We are indebted to Abhirup Sarkar and Sugata Marjit for their suggestions. This
paper was presented at The 1992 India and South-East Asia Meeting of the

(Continues...

presence of distortions, both in the domestic (rigid wages) as well as in the trade (tariffs) fronts, FTZs are shown to reduce the overall distortions. Economic welfare has been measured in terms of national income and the creation of FTZs has involved the reduction of tariffs on intermediate inputs. The literature[2] has also analysed the effects of trade policies on foreign exchange earnings for less developed countries that export traditional goods and which face adverse export demand elasticities. This paper tries to integrate these two strands by analysing the effects of creating FTZs on the foreign exchange constraint for an economy that is demand constrained at home and faces adverse export demand elasticities for its traditional exports.

Accordingly the paper is designed as follows: following the Introduction, Section 8.2 presents the model. Certain basic relationships are derived in Section 8.3, which are used in the comparative static exercises that follow. Section 8.4 analyses the effects of creating FTZs *vis-à-vis* fiscal measures and other export-oriented measures on the intensity of the foreign exchange constraint as well as on employment. A welfare analysis is presented in Section 8.5 and Section 8.6 concludes the paper.

8.2   The Model

We consider an open economy with two sectors, a traditional sector and a free trade zone, represented by indices u and f respectively. While both the goods are traded, the traditional exports are large whereas the free trade zone exports are small. Good f is produced in the FTZ with domestic labour, foreign capital and an imported intermediate input M. Good u is produced in the traditional sector with domestic labour, domestic capital and M. Whereas domestic labour and M are assumed to be perfectly mobile across sectors u and f, capital is assumed to be sector-specific. We also assume that the output of the traditional sector is demand constrained and that the nominal wages and the exchange rate are fixed.

Since the output of the FTZ is small there is no loss of generality if we normalize all international prices to be equal to unity.[3] Assuming

---

(Contd. ...

Econometric Society held at the Indira Gandhi Institute of Development Research, Bombay in December 1992, and at the Workshop on Issues in Development Economics in Jadavpur University, Calcutta in March 1993, and has benefited from the discussions. However, the usual disclaimer applies.

constant returns to scale in production, we can then write down the zero profit condition as

$$1 = C_f [w, R^*, (1 + T_f)e] \tag{8.1}$$

where w is the nominal wage rate, R^* is the returns to foreign capital, T_f is the tariff rate on M used in this sector, e is the exchange rate and C_f is the unit cost function. Since e is fixed and we will not be considering the effects of devaluation, here onwards we will take e to be equal to unity ($e \equiv 1$).

Let C_{Kf}, C_{Lf}, and C_{Mf} be the unit requirements of capital, labour and the imported intermediate input in sector f. By the Shephard–Samuelson relations, these can be obtained by differentiating the unit cost function with respect to the corresponding factor prices. As in Young (1987) we assume that there is an upward sloping supply curve $K^*(R^*)$ of foreign capital, i.e. $\partial K^* / \partial R^* > 0$. Full employment of foreign capital implies that

$$C_{Kf} X_f = K^* (R^*) \tag{8.2}$$

from which we can infer X_f. Employment in sector f is then $L_f = C_{Lf} X_f$.

We assume that the traditional sector is demand constrained and following Dutta (1984), Rakhshit (1989), Dornbusch (1980) and Taylor (1983), we further assume that the price of the traditional good, P_u, is fixed by applying a mark-up over unit costs,[4] i.e.

$$P_u = (1 + q) (wC_{Lu} + P_M C_{Mu}) \tag{8.3}$$

where q is the mark-up rate and P_M is the price of the imported input for the traditional sector. C_{Lu} and C_{Mu} are the unit requirements of labour and the imported input in u assumed to be exogenously given.

Effective demand for the traditional good, X_u^d, is

$$X_u^d = w (L_u + L_f)/P_u + (1 - s) R_u / P_u + Z + E_u (P_u) \tag{8.4}$$

where R_u and s are the profit income and saving propensity respectively of the domestic owners of capital, Z is real autonomous demand and $E_u(.)$ is the export demand function with $E_u' < 0$. Actual output, X_u, of the traditional sector then is given by

$$X_u^d = X_u \tag{8.5}$$

The foreign exchange constraint is incorporated by assuming that imports are determined by exports. The economy cannot run down

its foreign exchange reserves further and it cannot borrow from the international market. Our interpretation of a binding foreign exchange constraint is that, given the supply of imports, the domestic demand is such that the domestic price of imports is greater than the international price (multiplied by e).
We thus have

$$M^s = X_f + P_u E_u(P_u) - K^*(R^*)R^* \qquad (8.6)$$

M^s being the supply of the imported input.

The setting is as follows. The economy is large enough to determine the price of its traditional exports, but takes the international price of X_f and M as given. However, producers in the traditional sector pay a greater price for intermediate imports than is paid by the FTZ. The incentive that the FTZ enjoys is that the price of the intermediate import is kept lower here through conscious policy measures.

The domestic demand for the imported input, M^d, is given by

$$M^d = C_{Mf}X_f + C_{Mu} X_u^d \qquad (8.7)$$

and the equilibrium condition is

$$M^s = M^d = M \qquad (8.8)$$

The solution of the model is as follows. Eqn. (8.1) yields R^* and eqn. (8.2) yields X_f. This in turn yields L_f. So output and employment of the FTZ is determined independently of the traditional sector. It also fixes its own requirement of the imported intermediate input. Substituting for P_u in eqn. (8.4) and X_u^d in eqn. (8.7) yields a relationship between M_d and P_M. This is the derived effective demand schedule for the imported input. Again substituting for P_u in eqn. (8.6) yields a relationship between M^s and P_M. This is the supply schedule of the intermediate input. Eqn. (8.8), together with eqns. (8.6) and (8.7), determine the equilibrium values of M and P_M. The actual output of the traditional sector is then given by eqn. (8.5).

8.3   The Basic Relationships

This section derives the effective demand and supply schedules of the imported input, M.
From eqn. (8.4) we have

$$X_u^d = \frac{Z + E_u(P_u) + WL_f / P_u}{g+h}$$ (8.9)

where $g = sq / (1 + q)$ and $h = P_M C_{Mu} / Pu$.

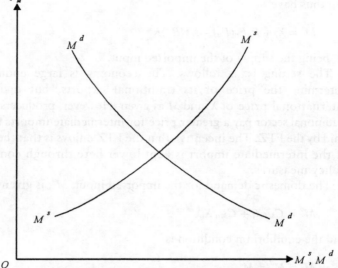

Fig. 8.1. Effective demand ($M^d M^d$) and supply ($M^s M^s$) schedules for M when $|E| < 1$.

It can be checked from eqns. (8.3) and (8.9) that $\partial X_u^d / \partial PM < 0$ and consequently from eqn. (8.7) that $\partial M^d / \partial P_M < 0$. That is, the derived effective demand schedule for the imported intermediate input is downward sloping. On the other hand, substituting for P_u in eqn. (8.6) and differentiating, yields

$$\partial M^s / \partial P_M = E_u(1 + E)(1 + q)C_{Mu}$$

where $E = (\partial E_u / \partial P_u).(P_u / E_u)$ is the price elasticity of demand for exports. So the supply schedule for the intermediate input is upward (downward) sloping if and only if $|E|$ is less (greater) than unity. From the demand and the supply schedules it can be inferred that the movement of excess demand for M with respect to P_M is given by

$$\partial(M^d - M^s)/\partial P_M = C_{Mu}^2 (1 + q)/(g + h) \ [E_u' - w(L_f + L_u)/P_u^2 - E_u(1 + E)(g + h)/C_{Mu}] = A \ (\text{say})$$

If $|E| < 1$, then A is necessarily negative. That is, the system is stable. If $|E| > 1$, then A is not necessarily negative. However, here onwards, we will assume stability, i.e. $A < 0$ (Figures 8.1 and 8.2).

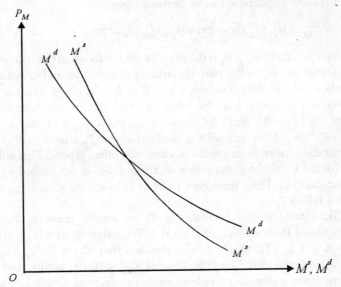

Fig. 8.2 Effective demand ($M^d M^d$) and supply ($M^s M^s$) schedules for M when $|E| > 1$.

8.4   Policy Analysis

We will now analyse the effects of creating a FTZ *vis-à-vis* the effects of fiscal- and export-oriented measures on the intensity of the foreign exchange constraint and on employment. One observation that should be kept in mind is that the foreign exchange constraint becomes increasingly tighter if P_M increases.

8.4.1   Creating a FTZ

It has already been shown that the variables pertaining to the FTZ can be solved independently of the traditional sector. Since w is given, from eqn. (8.1), a reduction in T_f increases R^*. This would raise the supply of foreign capital K^*. Totally differentiating eqn. (8.2) we get

$$\hat{X}_f + \hat{C}_{Kf} = e_{R^*} \, \hat{R}^* \tag{8.8}$$

where $e_{R*} \equiv dK^*/dR^*$. R^*/K^* is positive and $\equiv dz/z$ for any variable z. The total effect of the tariff decrease (comprising the direct effect plus the induced change in the returns to capital) on the unit requirement for capital can be derived from

$$\hat{C}_{Kf} = \theta_{Lf} S^f_{LK} (\hat{W} - \hat{R}^*) + \theta_{Mf} S^f_{MK} (\hat{T}_f - \hat{R}^*),$$

where $T_f = dT_f/(1 + T_f)$, θ_{ij} is the share of the i th factor in the costs of the j th sector and S^j_{in} is the partial elasticity of substitution between the inputs i and n in the jth sector, $i, n = K, L, M ; j = r, u, f$. Assume that capital is a substitute both for labour and for the intermediate input. Since $\hat{W}/\hat{T}_f = 0$ and $\hat{R}^*/\hat{T}_f = -\theta_{Mf}/\theta_{Kf} < 0$, it follows that $\hat{C}_{Kf}/\hat{T}_f > 0$. That is, with a reduction in T_f, there will be a substitution away from capital towards the other inputs. This will be reinforced by the indirect effect of an increase in R^* caused by the reduction in T_f. Thus, from eqn. (8.8), it follows that X_f will increase with a fall in T_f.

The effect of this increase in X_f on employment L_f can be determined from $L_f = C_{Lf} X_f$, total differentiation of which yields $\hat{L}_f = \hat{C}_{Lf} + \hat{X}_f$. Further it can be checked that $\hat{C}_{Lf} = \hat{T}_f \theta_{Mf} (S^f_{ML} - S^f_{KL})$. It follows that L_f will increase if $S^f_{ML} < 0$, i.e. labour and the intermediate input are complements in production. Employment in the FTZ can still increase if labour and the intermediate input are substitutes, i.e. $S^f_{ML} > 0$, provided that either this substitution effect is dominated by the effect of substitution from capital towards labour due to the rise in the price of capital or if $\left|\hat{X}_f/\hat{T}_f\right| > \left|\hat{C}_{Lf}/\hat{T}_f\right|$.

Proposition 1:   (a) If capital is a substitute for both labour and the imported input then a movement toward a FTZ will increase X_f.

(b) If $S^f_{ML} < 0$, or if $S^f_{KL} > S^f_{ML} > 0$, or if $\left|\hat{X}_f/\hat{T}_f\right| > \left|\hat{C}_{Lf}/\hat{T}_f\right|$., then a movement towards a FTZ will increase employment there.

The intuition behind Proposition 1 is as follows. When the tariff rate on the imported input is reduced, the rate of return on foreign capital increases. Then, on one hand, demand for capital per unit of output will decrease as other inputs will be substituted for capital. On the other hand, the supply of foreign capital will increase. For both reasons, output of the FTZ will expand [Proposition 1 (a)].

Employment in the FTZ would increase due to an expansion of output in the zone and the substitution of labour for capital. If the imported input and labour are complements in production, then a fall in the tariff rate on imported input will lead to an increase in use of labour by the zone. So employment will necessarily increase. Again, if imported input and labour are substitutes then such a reduction in the tariff rate will lead to a substitution away from labour and a fall in employment. However, if the extent of substitutability between the imported input and labour is less than that between foreign capital and labour, or if the expansionary effect on employment due to expansion in output outweighs the substitution effect, then employment in the FTZ will increase [Proposition 1 (b)].

For determining the effects of a reduction in T_f on the employment in the traditional sector, we substitute eqns. (8.2), (8.3), (8.6), (8.7) and (8.9) in eqn. (8.8), total differentiation of which yields

$$dP_m / dT_f = [dX_f / dT_f - d(K^*R^*) / dT_f - d(C_{Mf} X_f) / dT_f$$
$$- \{C_{Mu}{}^w / P_u(g + h)\} dL_f / dT_f] / A$$

The first two terms in the right-hand side of the above expression represent a net shift in the supply schedule of the intermediate input and the last two terms represent a shift in the demand schedule for the intermediate input.

Further, substituting eqn. (8.9) in (8.5) and totally differentiating yields

$$dX_u / dT_f = (\partial X_u / \partial L_f).(dL_f / dT_f) + (\partial X_u / \partial PM).(dP_M / dT_f)$$

where $\partial X_u / \partial L_f > 0$ and $\partial X_u / \partial P_M < 0$.
Since A is negative, we have

Proposition 2:   A movement towards a FTZ will
(a) tighten the foreign exchange constraint if the demand curve for the intermediate input shifts more than the supply curve;
(b) increase aggregate output and employment of the economy if the foreign exchange constraint becomes less binding and if Proposition 1. (b) holds.

Given Proposition 1, the general equilibrium effects of creating a FTZ can be analysed through: (i) the effect of increase in output of the FTZ on the demand for the imported input; (ii) the effect of substituting the imported input for other inputs in the FTZ; (iii) the effects of increasing L_f on effective demand for the traditional good and hence on the derived demand for the imported input; and (iv) the effect of increasing X_f and R^* on the supply of the imported input.

For Proposition 2 it may be noted that the first three effects will lead to a shift to the right in the derived demand schedule for the imported input and the fourth effect will lead to a shift to the right in the supply schedule of the imported input. It is obvious that the domestic price of the imported input will increase (decrease) if the demand curve shifts more (less) than the supply curve [Proposition 2(a)]. The intuition behind Proposition 2(b) can be similarly derived.

8.4.2 Change in Z

The general equilibrium effects of a change in autonomous demand can be derived by substituting eqns. (8.3), (8.6), (8.7) and (8.9) in (8.8) and totally differentiating it. This would yield

$$dP_M / dz = - C_{Mu} / (g + h) A > 0.$$

Again substituting eqn. (8.9) in (8.5) and totally differentiating yields

$$dX_u / dZ = - [E_u(1 + E) / C_{Mu}] / [E_u' - w(L_f + L_u) / P_u^2 - E_u$$
$$(1 + E)(g + h)/C_{Mu}]$$

This yields the following proposition.

Proposition 3:   If real autonomous expenditure increases, then the domestic price of the imported input will necessarily increase. Output and employment of the FTZ will remain unaffected. Aggregate output and employment of the economy will increase if $|E|$ is less than unity or if $|E|$ is greater than unity, but the system is stable.

It may be noted that the output and employment of the FTZ will not be affected if there is a change in Z. But effective demand and consequently derived demand for the imported input will change due to a change in Z. If real autonomous expenditure increases, then the effective demand for and hence the output of the traditional sector will increase. Thus the derived demand schedule for the imported input will shift towards the right; on the other hand, the supply schedule of the imported input will remain unchanged. So the domestic price of imported input will increase. The effect of increase in Z on output and employment of the traditional sector will, however, in addition depend upon the elasticity of demand for traditional exports.

8.4.3 Change in C_{Lu}

Substituting eqns. (8.3), (8.6), (8.7) and (8.9) in (8.8) and totally differentiating yields

$$dP_M / dC_{Lu} = [C_{Mu} (1 + q)w / (g + h)][E_u (1 + E)(g + h) / C_{Mu} -$$
$$E + WL_f/P_u^2 + X_u C_{Mu} P_M / (g + h)P_u^2] / A$$

We thus have

Proposition 4:   If the requirement of labour per unit of output falls in the traditional sector, then the foreign exchange constraint will become tighter if $|E| < 1$. Aggregate output and employment of the economy as a whole will, however, necessarily increase.

The above proposition requires explanation. Due to labour augmenting technical progress in the traditional sector, i.e., a fall in C_{Lu}, P_u would fall from eqn. (8.3). This, given $|E| < 1$ will reduce export earnings and consequently, the availability of imports. Thus, given P_M, the supply schedule M^s would shift to the left. Again, a fall in P_u would increase effective demand and, given P_M, would shift the M_d schedule to the right. Thus, P_M would necessarily increase checking a part of the initial fall in P_u. However, in the final equilibrium, P_u would be lower and hence effective demand would be higher and so would output and employment in the traditional sector. As the FTZ remains unaffected, output and employment in the economy as a whole would increase.

8.5   Welfare Analysis

For welfare calculations we take national income, Y, as the index of welfare, where

$$Y = w (L_u + L_f) + q(C_{Lu} w + C_{Mu} P_M) X_u + M_f T_f \qquad 8.10$$

The first term is total wage income, the second term is the income of the domestic owners of capital, and the third term is tariff income.

8.5.1   Creation of a FTZ

Totally differentiating eqn. (8.10) we have

$$dY / dT_f = \{(1 + q)C_{Lu} w + qC_{Mu} P_M\} dX_u / dT_f + w(dL_f / dT_f)$$
$$+ qC_{Mu} X_u (dP_m / dT_f) + M_f (1 + E_{Mf})$$

where $E_{Mf} = (dM_f / dT_f)T_f / M_f$ is the elasticity of demand for the imported input in the FTZ with respect to the tariff rate. Given that $M_f = C_{Mf} X_f$, it can be checked that $E_{Mf} < 0$.

The conditions determining the signs of dX_u / dT_f, dL_f / dT_f and dP_M / dT_f can be obtained from Proposition 1 and 2.

This suggests the following proposition.

Proposition 5:   Creation of a FTZ will increase welfare if Proposition 2(b) holds and if $|E_{Mf}| > 1$.

8.5.2 Change in Z

Totally differentiating eqn. (8.10) yields

$$dY/dZ = \{(1 + q)C_{Lu} + qC_{Mu}P_M\}dX_u / dZ + qC_{Mu}X_u dP_M / dZ$$

We thus have the following proposition.

Proposition 6: An increase in autonomous expenditure will improve welfare if Proposition 3 holds.

An interested reader can derive the welfare effects of technical progress in the traditional sector along the lines suggested above.

8.6 Conclusion

This paper develops an analytical framework in terms of which the effects of creating FTZs on the foreign exchange constraint can be analysed. Further, these effects can be compared to the effects of fiscal measures and other measures like technological change in the traditional sector. It can be inferred from the analysis that, in an economy facing adverse export demand elasticities, if FTZs increase aggregate output and employment, it would improve the foreign exchange situation. Compared to this, technical progress in the traditional sector, in spite of increasing aggregate output and employment, will worsen the foreign exchange situation.

On comparing the effects of an expansion of FTZs with the effects of an increase in autonomous demand we find that, although the latter will have expansionary effects in terms of income and employment in the presence of adverse export elasticity conditions, the foreign exchange constraint will become necessarily tighter. In contrast, the expansionary effects of creating a FTZ will be accompanied by an easing of the foreign exchange constraint.

Notes

1. See Young (1987), Young and Miyagiwa (1987), Beladi and Marjit (1992a, 1992b) and Datta Chaudhuri and Adhikary (1993).
2. See Desai and Bhagwati (1979), Chenery and Bruno (1962), Mackinnon (1964) and Findlay (1971).
3. The production of the good produced in the FTZ is small relative to the world production and, hence, the country cannot influence the world price of the good by changing the level of production; in that case the international price of good f is fixed.

4. We can use the marginal cost pricing rule. However, a mark-up pricing rule simplifies the algebra significantly without loss of any significant interaction among the variables. Only, the substitution effects among the inputs in the traditional sector drop out.

References

Beladi, H. and S. Marjit. (1992a). Foreign capital and protectionism. *Canadian Journal of Economics* 25, 1: 233–238.

——— (1992b). Foreign capital, unemployment and national welfare. *Japan and the World Economy* 4, 4: 311–317.

Chenery, H. and M. Bruno. (1962). Development alternatives in an open economy : the case of Israel. *Economic Journal* 72: 79–103.

Datta Chaudhuri, T. and S. Adhikary. (1993). Free trade zones with Harris–Todaro unemployment: a note on Young–Miyagiwa. *Journal of Development Economics* 41: 157–162.

Desai, P. and J. Bhagwati. (1979). Three alternative concepts of foreign exchange difficulties in centrally planned economies. *Oxford Economic Papers*, 358–368.

Dornbusch, R. (1980). *Open Economy Macroeconomics*. New York: Basic Books.

Dutta, A. K. (1984). Stagnation, income distribution and monopoly power. *Cambridge Journal of Economics* 8: 25–40.

Findlay, R. (1971). The foreign exchange gap and growth in developing economies. In *Trade, Balance of Payments and Growth*, ed. J. Bhagwati et al. Amsterdam: North Holland Co.

Mackinnon, R. (1964). Foreign exchange constraints in economic development and efficient aid allocation. *Economic Journal*, 388–409.

Rakshit, M. (1989). *Studies in the Macroeconomics of Developing Countries*. New Delhi: Oxford University Press.

Taylor, L. (1983). *Structuralist Macroeconomics*. New York: Basic Books.

Young, L. (1987). Intermediate goods and the formation of duty free zones. *Journal of Development Economics* 25: 369–384.

Young, L. and K. Miyagiwa. (1987). Unemployment and the formation of duty free zones. *Journal of Development Economics* 26: 397–405.

Gains from Full and Partial Liberalization Under Duopoly

Joysri Banerji Acharyya[*]

9.1 Introduction

Neo-classical trade theory has time and again emphasised unilateral free trade and the gains therefrom. Import liberalization has been demonstrated to be welfare-improving simply because of the consumption gain, even if there is no scope for production gain. In general it is argued that, import liberalization expands competition and competition is efficient.

The new trade theories replacing "passive" perfect competition with "active" competition, have been able to identify cases where the

---

[*] This paper is a revised version of the first chapter of my M.Phil. dissertation. I acknowledge my debt to my supervisor, Prof. Kalyan Kumar Sanyal, for his guidance. Thanks are also due to Bhaswar Moitra, Rajat Acharyya, Sanjoy Banerji and Sarmila Banerji for their valued comments and suggestions. However, the usual disclaimer applies.

Gains From Trade proposition is challenged. For example, when there are only few firms operating and interacting with each other in the global market, liberalization leads only to oligopolistic competition in the domestic market. In such a case the welfare implications of liberalization might run contrary to conventional wisdom. A re-examination of the gains to be had from liberalization in light of the new trade theories is, therefore, of utmost importance, particularly for the Less Developed Countries (LDCs) who have recently adopted liberalization.

This is exactly what we attempt here. In particular, we examine the welfare implications of liberalization under duopoly with a single home and foreign firm selling a homogeneous good in the erstwhile protected home market. However, we adopt a Conjectural Variation (CV) approach (Bresnahan 1981; Perry 1982) rather than specific conjectures like Cournot, Bertrand, or Stackelberg. This approach is motivated firstly by the Bhagwati (1988) observation, that policy recommendations are sensitive to behavioural assumptions and secondly by Hwang-Mai's (1988) demonstration, that the equivalence of tariff and quota depends on the value of CV.

In Section 9.2 we present the model and examine the welfare effects of liberalization. Section 9.3 compares partial liberalization (restricted trade), with full liberalization (free trade) and no liberalization (autarky) in welfare terms. In Section 9.4 we consider an alternative model of ministerial evaluation of liberalization and re-examine welfare issues. Concluding remarks appear in Section 9.5.

9.2   The Model

Consider a domestic market with a single firm producing a homogeneous good "X", so that under autarky the market is monopolized by the firm. When the import regime is liberalized, a foreign firm producing the same good at a plant located in its own country, enters the domestic market and sells the product competing with the home firm, i.e., after liberalization we have duopoly. We assume both firms to be quantity setters and instead of assuming a particular behaviour we adopt a conjectural variation (CV) approach. Value of CV, 'r' defined as one firm's conjecture about the slope of its rival's reaction function, may take any value within the range -1 and $+1$ in our duopoly case.

Different values of CV specifying the behavioural patterns, thus produce different oligopolistic solutions. For example, value of CV equal to -1, 0 and $+1$ yields "quasi-competitive" or Bertrand, Cournot, and (perfectly) collusive solutions respectively. Alternatively, a CV greater than zero implies a form of collusion, while a CV less than zero indicates a non-cooperative conduct.

Let the demand function in inverse form be

$$P = f(x) \; ; \; f' < 0; \; f'' < 0 \tag{9.1}$$

where $X = x + x^* = $ total supply of the good in the domestic market. We assume zero fixed costs and constant marginal costs (MC). The latter implies segmented markets, i.e., exports of the foreign firm in the home country, x^*, is independent of its sales in its own country. Denoting the MCs by c and c^* we get the following profit functions:

$$\pi = [f(X) - c] \, x \tag{9.2}$$

$$\pi^* = [f(X) - c^*] \, x^* \tag{9.3}$$

Let us assume identical costs, i.e., $c = c^*$. Now from the first-order condition for profit maximization we obtain the reaction functions of the two firms as follows:

$$R = R \, (x, x^*, r) \tag{9.4}$$

$$R^* = R^* \, (x, x^*, r) \tag{9.5}$$

where $r = dx_j / dx_k = dx_k / dx_j, \; k \neq j$ is the symmetric CV. These two reaction functions can be solved for the equilibrium output levels as follows:

$$\bar{x} = \bar{x}(r) \tag{9.6}$$

$$\bar{x}^* = \bar{x}^* \, (r) \tag{9.7}$$

Since MCs are identical and the conjectures are symmetric, domestic production $\bar{x}$ and import $\bar{x}^*$ under free trade are equal in magnitude. It can also be verified that,

$$\partial \bar{x} / \partial r < 0 \text{ and } \partial \bar{x}^* / \partial r < 0, \tag{9.8}$$

i.e., volume of import and hence domestic production are both inversely related to the value of CV, i.e., 'r'. This is because of the following reasons. With $r = -1$ we have the quasi-competitive solution and as 'r' rises in value, the solution tends to a collusive one. It is well-known that industry output is largest under competition and smallest when it is collusive. Since, the output of each firm is just half of the industry output, so it is least for $r = +1$ and maximum for $r = -1$.[1]

Accordingly, the equilibrium domestic price varies positively with 'r' given equation (9.1),

$$\bar{P} = P[X(r)] = P(r), \; P' > 0 \tag{9.9}$$

Finally, the domestic welfare level under free trade can be defined as the sum of the consumer's surplus $S(P)$ and the producer's surplus $\pi(x)$,

$$W = S(\bar{P}) + \pi(\bar{x}) \tag{9.10}$$

Since both the equilibrium price and the domestic output depend on 'r', so will the welfare level, i.e.,

$$W = W(r), \; \partial W / \partial r < 0 \tag{9.11}$$

Therefore we can write,

Proposition 1: Welfare under free trade varies inversely with the value of 'r'.

We can verify this in terms of Figure 9.1. $D'D'$ is the demand curve, 'c' represents the marginal cost *(MC)*. For $r = -1$, price equals 'c', profit equals zero and welfare equals area $D'AC$. As 'r' rises, total as

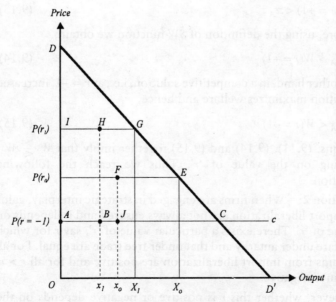

Fig. 9.1   Free trade welfare under different values of CV

well as the firm output falls and price rises as indicated by eqns. (9.8) and (9.9). Consider $r_0 > -1$: the price goes up to $P(r_0)$ and the total output falls to X_0 . Given $x_0 = \frac{1}{2}X_0$, welfare now equals the area $D'AJFE$ which is lower than the area $D'AC$. So welfare falls. In this way as we raise the value of 'r', welfare falls.

This is obvious. Actually, with $r = -1$, we have a MC pricing which is "efficient". But as 'r' increases in value, the market becomes more and more imperfect, i.e., the price rises higher and higher above MC, so that we deviate more and more from the Pareto optimal situation, and welfare falls.

Let us now turn to the gains to be had from liberalization. First of all, it should be noted that the autarkic output equals total output under free trade in collusive equilibrium, i.e., $r = +1$. Under autarky, the home firm is a monopolist, maximizing its profit, while a collusive solution under free trade is just the case of joint profit maximization. Therefore, the domestic price under the two alternative systems will also be same, so that

$$S(\overline{P}) = S(P_A) \tag{9.12}$$

But profit under autarky is equal to the sum of the profit of domestic and foreign firms under free trade at $r = +1$. Hence,

$$\pi(r = +1) < \pi_A \tag{9.13}$$

Therefore, using the definition of SW function we obtain,

$$W_A > W(r = +1) \tag{9.14}$$

On the other hand, in a competitive solution, i.e., at $r = -1$, increased competition maximizes welfare and hence,

$$W_A < W(r = -1) \tag{9.15}$$

Thus eqns. (9.11), (9.14) and (9.15) together imply that $W \gtrless W_A$, depending on the value of 'r'. Thus we reach the following proposition.

Proposition 2:   When firms are engaged in strategic interplay, gains from import liberalization are not always ensured and it depends on the value of 'r'. There exists a particular value of 'r', say $\bar{r}$ for which the welfare under autarky and that under free trade are equal. For all $r < \bar{r}$, gains from import liberalization are positive and for all $r > \bar{r}$, such gain is negative.

However, whether this $\bar{r}$ is positive or negative depends on the convexity of the $W(r)$ curve.

That import liberalization is not always beneficial can be explained as follows. Under import liberalization while due to increased competition consumers are benefited by a lower price of the good, the domestic producer enjoys a lower (duopoly) profit. That is we have two opposing forces at work: one is the favourable consumption effect, and the other is the negative profit leakage effect. Hence a positive gain from liberalization is not guaranteed. However, in a competitive environment the favourable effect dominates the negative effect and there are positive gains from liberalization. But, as 'r' increases in value from −1, the domestic market becomes less and less competitive under free trade so that the favourable consumption effect and hence the gains from liberalization become smaller and smaller in magnitude. And $\bar{r}$, is the value of CV for which the two opposite effects are equal at the margin.

Proposition 3:   For linear demand, $W = W(A)$ at $r = -1/3$, i.e., there are positive gains from import liberalization only for a restricted set of post-liberalization non-cooperative equilibria, i.e., for $-1 \leq r < 1/3$, as shown in Figure 9.2.

Proof: Let the linear demand be,

$$P = a - (x + x^*) \tag{9.16}$$

From first order profit-maximizing conditions we obtain the reaction functions

$$(2 + r) x_1 + x_2 = a - c \tag{9.17}$$

$$x_1 + (2 + r)x_2 = a - c \tag{9.18}$$

These can be solved for the equilibrium output levels as follows

$$\bar{x} = \bar{x}^* = (a - c) / (r + 3) \tag{9.19}$$

Substitution of values from eqn. (9.19) in eqn. (9.16) yields the equilibrium price

$$\bar{P} = [(1 + r)a + 2c] / (r + 3) \tag{9.20}$$

Finally, the free trade welfare level is calculated as,

$$W = (a - c)^2 / (r + 3) \tag{9.21}$$

By considering the autarkic position, the welfare under autarky is found to be

$$W(A) = 3(a - c)^2 / 8 \tag{9.22}$$

Equating eqns. (9.21) and (9.22) we obtain $r = -1/3$.

Interpreting autarky as prohibitive tariff it appears that there might be some tariff policy that may improve welfare, i.e., partial liberalization might be better. Let us now turn to this issue.

9.3   Partial Liberalization : The Tariff Case

Let us consider the move from autarky (or prohibitive tariff) to positive specific tariff, which implies partial liberalization in contrast to the full liberalization considered in the previous section. Such a movement has three effects: (i) positive revenue effect; (ii) positive consumption effect as price is reduced due to increased competition; and (iii) negative profit effect.

In a previous analysis, Brander and Spencer (1984) have demonstrated under Cournot conjecture that an optimum tariff exists, depending on the relative curvature of the demand curve. In terms of our linear demand curve analysis, it can be easily verified that their optimum tariff result holds for all non-Bertrand conjectures and that the value of such optimum specific tariff varies directly with the value of 'r',

$$\bar{t} = [(a - c)(1 + r)] / (3 + 2r) \tag{9.23}$$

Proposition 4:   Partial liberalization is superior to full liberalization for all non-Bertrand conjectures. This is illustrated in Figure 9.2.

Optimum tariff also exists when we replace specific tariff by an *ad valorem* tariff, 's'. Such an *ad valorem* tariff leads to the same domestic price and output but generates higher revenue for the government compared to the 'equal-import' specific tariff.

The equal-import *ad valorem* tariff, by definition, leaves unaffected the foreign firm's profit maximizing sales in the domestic market compared to a given specific tariff. That is, both the firms are left in the same strategic position *vis-à-vis* others under the two tariff systems. It is obvious then that equal-import *ad valorem* and specific tariffs will be price-equivalent.

That the tariff revenues, differ under two tariff systems, can be seen as follows. By definitions,

$$TR_s = s.P_s.x_{2s} \tag{9.24}$$

$$TR_t = t.x_{2t} \tag{9.25}$$

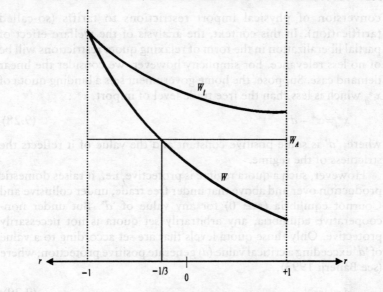

Fig. 9.2   Welfare ranking of full liberalization, partial liberalization and no-liberalization (autarky).

Now the relation between equal-import *ad valorem* and specific tariff is given as

$$t = cs / (1 - s) \tag{9.26}$$

This relation is obtained from $P_t = P_s$. Then,

$$TR_t - TR_s = s.x_{2s} \left[\frac{c}{(1-s)} - P_s \right] \tag{9.27}$$

Now, as the non-negative profit constraint implies $(1 - s). Ps > c$ so $TR_t < TR_s$ for $r \neq -1$. From this proposition 5 follows.

Proposition 5:   Given linear demand and constant marginal costs, *ad valorem* tariff is superior to an equal import specific tariff for all non-Bertrand conjectures.

Therefore, we observe that not only is there a clear choice between partial liberalization and full liberalization in a strategic model like this but also that there is a choice between modes of such partial liberalization.

9.3.1   Quota reduction and tariffication

The eighth round of multilateral trade negotiations, popularly known as the Uruguay Round, contained the mandate to negotiate on the conversion of physical import restrictions to tariffs (so-called tariffication). In this context, the analysis of the welfare effect of partial liberalization in the form of relaxing quota restrictions will be of no less relevance. For simplicity however, we consider the linear demand case. Suppose, the home government sets a binding quota of x^*_q which is less than the free trade level of import, x^* :

$$x^*_q = x^* - d \tag{9.28}$$

where, 'd' is some positive constant and the value of it reflects the strictness of the regime.

However, such a quota regime is protective, i.e., it raises domestic production over and above that under free trade, under collusive and Cournot equilibria ($r \geq 0$) for any value of 'd'. But under non-cooperative equilibria, any arbitrarily set quota is not necessarily protective. Only those quota levels that are set according to a value of 'd' exceeding a critical value ($\overline{d}$) generate positive protection, where (see Banerji 1993),

$$\overline{d} = |rx^*| \tag{9.29}$$

Now, given the linear demand function eqn. (9.16), the welfare level under a quota system can be calculated as

$$W_q = [(24 + 16r + 3r^2)(a-c)^2 + 3d^2(r+3)^2 +$$
$$2dr(r+3)(a-c)] / 8(r+3)^2 \tag{9.30}$$

Comparing eqn. (9.21) and (9.30) we observe,

$$W_q > W \qquad \forall \; r > 0 \tag{9.31}$$

$$W_q < W \qquad \forall \; r < 0,$$

where the welfare ranking for $r < 0$ is obtained by using eqn. (9.29). Proposition 6 follows.

Proposition 6: Abolition of the quota regime in a duopolistic environment raises welfare only under non-cooperative equilibria.

Now, from eqn. (9.30) it is also evident that welfare under the quota regime depends also on the strictness of the regime, i.e., on the value of 'd'. Differentiating eqn. (9.30) partially with respect to 'd' we obtain,

$$\partial W_q / \partial d > 0 \qquad \forall \; r > 0 \tag{9.32a}$$

Thus, under cooperative equilibria W_q is a monotonic increasing function of the quota level. That is, the stricter the quota regime, the greater is the welfare. Under non-cooperative equilibria, on the other hand, we observe,

$$\partial Wq \, / \, \partial d \gtreqless 0 \quad \text{as } d \gtreqless d_0 \qquad (9.32b)$$

where,

$$d_0 = - \, rx^* \, / \, 3 \qquad (9.33)$$

It is interesting that the maximum welfare under the quota regime equals the welfare under free trade in Cournot equilibrium:

$$W_q \, (d_0) = W \, (r = 0)$$

Therefore, we arrive at the next proposition.

Proposition 7:   For Cournot and cooperative solutions relaxation of quota restrictions necessarily lowers welfare. But for non-cooperative equilibria, all depends on the initial quota level. If the initial quota level is such that $d > d_0$, successive quota reduction will first raise welfare and then will reduce it, though in any case welfare will be lower than under free trade as is evident from Proposition 6.

In sum, the abolition or reduction of quota restrictions is not necessarily welfare improving in a duopoly.

9.4   The Model of Ministerial Evaluation

Any trade policy affects consumers and producers dissimilarly. This points to a conflict in attitudes of these interacting classes towards a particular trade policy. In a democratic setting, where decision making is often influenced by political forces and pressure groups, such a conflict in attitudes cannot be altogether neglected. Often the government and the policymakers also do not remain indifferent to these opposing interest groups and favour one or the other group. One way to capture this fact within our policy framework is to redefine the social welfare function in the following way:

$$W = S(P) + m. \, \pi \, (x) + n.TR, \quad (m, \, n \geq 0), \qquad (9.34)$$

where the values of 'm' and 'n' reflect relative importance or weights placed on different components of the social welfare function. For example, in the presence of a powerful producers' (or consumers') lobby we can expect a value of 'm' greater (less) than unity in the evaluation of trade policies. Similarly, in an *LDC*, facing resource constraint policymakers may well put a greater weight on revenues earned from a trade policy, i.e., $n > m$ and $n > 1$.

In other words, while the SW function with $m = n = 1$, can be regarded as the social planners' evaluation, the SW function defined in eqn. (9.34), represents the ministerial evaluation which may be identical with the former only when election strategies lead to putting unit (or equal) values to 'm' and 'n'. In general, the value of 'm' and 'n' captures the "bias" of the government against or in favour of a particular group of people or economic agent while approving a policy.

Now the welfare levels under autarky and free trade can be rewritten in the general form as,

$$W_A = W_A(\overline{m}), \quad W'_A = PS_A > 0 \tag{9.35}$$

and

$$W = W(\overline{m}, r), \quad \partial W / \partial r < 0, \quad \partial W / \partial m = PS > 0 \tag{9.36}$$

Equating eqns. (9.35) and (9.36) we obtain

$$d\overline{m} / dr = \frac{\partial W / dr}{(\pi_A - \pi)} < 0 \tag{9.37}$$

Proposition 8: The welfare ranking of autarky and free trade depends on the value of 'm' and this value of 'm' varies inversely with the value of the CV as indicated by equation (9.37).

In the linear case, the welfare levels under autarky and free trade can be obtained as

$$W_A = (1 + 2m)(a - c)^2 / 8 \tag{9.38}$$

$$W = [2 + (1 + r)m](a - c)^2 / (3 + r)^2 \tag{9.39}$$

Subtracting eqn. (9.38) from (9.39) we get

$$W - W_A \gtreqless 0 \text{ as } m \lesseqgtr \frac{7 - r(6 + r)}{2[5 + r(2 + r)]} \tag{9.40}$$

In particular, under the Bertrand conjecture ($r = -1$) positive gains from liberalization arise for $m < 1.5$, whereas under the Cournot conjecture and for collusive equilibrium the gains arise for $m < 0.7$ and $m = 0$ respectively. The noteworthy point is that for a sufficiently larger weight placed on consumers' surplus, trade liberalization is beneficial under Cournot and co-operative equilibria unlike in the previous case.

9.5   Conclusions

The above analysis demonstrates that in an oligopolistic environment gains from liberalization are not necessarily positive. For a non-linear demand curve, the range of CV for which gains from liberalization are positive depends on the convexity of the demand curve. Thus, if the government can make a choice between alternative trade regimes and has information about firm behaviour, it should liberalize the import regime only for values of CV not exceeding some critical level $\bar{r}$, which in the linear demand case equals $-1/3$. However, the government often does not have any information about firm behaviour, or the import regime is liberalized for considerations other than social welfare. The above analysis then shows the costs of liberalization. However, tariff-restricted trade or partial liberalization is superior to autarky as well as full liberalization. In particular, under cooperative equilibria, full liberalization is certainly Pareto–inferior to both partial and no-liberalization. Choice between partial and no-liberalization, on the other hand, depends on the nature of the restricted trade regime. The first-best policy is attained when the economy is partially liberalized by replacing the autarkic, or the prohibitive tariff, regime by an (optimum) tariff-restricted regime. But partial liberalization in the form of quota-restricted regime, although welfare improving when compared to full liberalization, is found to be Pareto–inferior to no-liberalization. Hence, a quota regime is only the third-best policy. This means that under co-operative equilibria, conversion of quotas into tariffs will help the economy to maximize its welfare and seems to be the right kind of policy. But successive reduction of tariff rates are certainly welfare reducing.

On comparing situations under non-cooperative equilibria with that under cooperative equilibria, we make the following observations. First, the welfare ranking of no-liberalization and full liberalization depends on the value of CV. Second, abolition of the quotas regime raises welfare only under the non-cooperative equilibria. Our third observation is that the welfare effects of conversion of quotas into tariffs, commonly called "tariffication", and of reduction of tariff rates are qualitatively the same.

Finally, in a model of ministerial evaluation, we have found that welfare rankings of alternative trade policies depend upon the specification of the social welfare function.

The above analyses can be extended to a few important directions. On the one hand, the cost asymmetric analyses may be incorporated, which might have quite different welfare implications as have been observed by Acharyya and Marjit (1994) and Kabiraj (1994). On the other hand, with endogenously determined weights on different components of social welfare function, in terms of lobbying efforts put by different pressure groups, we can focus on the political economy of liberalization.

Notes

1. The equilibrium here is essentially a non-cooperative one and hence is self-enforcing. The nomenclature of co-operative conduct (r > 0) by Bresnahan (1981) and others actually means tacit collusion in the sense that each player's action would be exactly duplicated by the other players, though they do not explicitly enter into any binding contract. See also Kolstad and Wolak (1986), Perry (1982).

References

Acharyya, R. and S. Marjit. (1994). Game of entry with an inefficient incumbent: The case of import liberalization in developing countries. Working Paper.

Banerji, J. (1993). Welfare implications of free trade and alternative trade policies in a strategic model : A conjectural variation approach. M.Phil. dissertation, University of Calcutta.

Bhagwati, J.N. (1988). *Protectionism*. Massachusetts: MIT Press.

Brander, J.A. (1981). Intra-industry trade in identical commodities. *Journal of International Economics* 11: 1–14.

Brander, J.A. and B.J.Spencer. (1984). Trade warfare: Tariffs and Cartels. *Journal of International Economics* 16: 227–242.

Bresnahan, T.F. (1981). Duopoly Models with Consistent Conjectures. *American Economic Review* 71: 934–945.

Eaton, J. and G.M.Grossman. (1986). Optimal trade and industrial policy under oligopoly. *Quarterly Journal of Economics* 101: 383–406.

Helpman, E. and P. Krugman. (1989). *Trade Policy and Market Structure*. Massachusetts: MIT Press.

Hwang, H. and C. Mai. (1988). On the equivalence of tariffs and quotas under duopoly. *Journal of International Economics* 24: 373–380.

Kabiraj, T. (1994). Free trade vs autarky — A welfare analysis. *The Indian Economic Journal* 41: 165–169.

Kolstad, C.D. and F.A. Wolak. (1986). Conjectural variation and the indeterminacy of duopolistic equilibria. *Canadian Journal of Economics* XIX, 4: 656–677.

Perry, M. (1982). Oligopoly and consistent conjectural variation. *Bell Journal of Economics* 13: 197–205.

Sen, A. (1990). Privatisation and social welfare. Discussion Paper No. 32, Goregaon, Bombay: Indira Gandhi Institute of Development Research.

Exit Policy, Post-Liberalization Game Between Cost Asymmetric Home and Foreign Firms and Welfare

Rajat Acharyya[*]

10.1 Introduction

Firms in the less developed countries (LDCs) often have high cost structures when compared to international standards and this

* This is a shorter and revised version of the paper presented at the IV Annual Conference on Contemporary Issues in Development Economics organized by the Department of Economics, Jadavpur University during 2–3 September, 1994. I wish to thank Avirup Sarkar, Sugata Marjit, seminar discussant Sarmila Banerji and the editors of this volume for their valued comments and suggestions. I have also benefited from the discussion with Kaushik Basu on an earlier draft. The usual disclaimer applies, however.

influences in a large part the post-entry strategy of the foreign firms and the post-entry game when the erstwhile protected domestic market is liberalized. This has some far reaching implications for the gains to be had from liberalization. Kabiraj (1994), for example, has observed that such gains depend on the degree of cost difference when the post-liberalization game is Cournot. On the other hand, Acharyya and Marjit (1994) have demonstrated that the foreign entrant's decision to accommodate or throw out the high-cost incumbent depends crucially on how inefficient the incumbent is.

However, along with the high cost structure of the LDC-firms, often a large part of their costs are "sunk" due to many institutional factors. For example, firms in LDCs cannot employ a hire-and-fire policy or what in the Indian context is known as the "exit" policy. As a result, labour retrenchment is virtually impossible at least in the short run.[1] This "policy constraint" together with the capacity constraints, another common observation in the LDCs, may change the whole post-liberalization game with quite different welfare implications. This is what motivates us to reconsider the post-liberalization game. In Section 10.2 we spell out the model and describe the autarkic equilibrium. Section 10.3 discusses the post-liberalization game and the welfare results in the absence of the exit policy. In Section 10.4 we examine the role of the exit policy and the degree of cost asymmetry. Finally, Section 10.5 concludes the paper.

10.2   The Model and the Autarkic Equilibrium

Consider a capacity constrained domestic firm producing a good, I, in the protected home market at zero fixed cost and constant marginal cost (MC), c, up to the capacity level. The MC has two parts: marginal material cost, c^r, and marginal labour cost, c^L. This is the case as long as labour can be fired as and when necessary. But in the LDCs such a hire-and-fire (or "exit") policy cannot be followed. Labour retrenchments are virtually impossible and labour costs become "sunk". In such a case $c = c^r$ and $c^L \cdot \bar{x} = S$ is the sunk cost which cannot be avoided by shutting down.

We also assume that the firm is capacity constrained, i.e., it cannot increase output beyond a particular level, $\bar{x}$. This is not hard to justify in the context of a LDC-firm. In the LDCs the capacity is often given exogenously, i.e., due to factors beyond its control, it is not chosen by the firm. For example, there are infrastructural bottlenecks, input supply rigidities, energy inefficiencies and the like, which we can call "structural constraints". In formulating the model we have in our mind such a structurally constrained firm. However, without any loss of generality we assume that the capacity output equals monopoly output for $c = c^r$:

$$\bar{x} = x_m(c^r) \tag{10.1}$$

This is to keep things simple and to facilitate welfare comparisons.

Thus the autarkic equilibrium is the standard monopoly equilibrium both in the presence or absence of a hire-and-fire or exit policy. The only difference is that given our assumption about capacity level, when an exit policy exists there will be some unutilised capacity. Assuming a linear demand function of the form,

$$p = a - X, a > 0 \tag{10.2}$$

where p is the domestic price, and X is the total supply, the solutions are given as:

$$x_A = X_A = (a - c) / 2 \tag{10.3}$$

$$P_A = (a + c) / 2 \tag{10.4}$$

$$\Pi_A = (a - c)^2 / 4 \tag{10.5}$$

$$W_A = 3(a - c)^2 / 8 \tag{10.6}$$

where, $c = c^r + c^L$ when the exit policy can be applied, $c = c^r$ when it cannot be applied, and W denotes social welfare defined as the sum of the consumers' surplus and the home firm's profit.

10.3   The Post-Liberalization Game

Consider a foreign firm producing the same good at a plant located in its own country at a marginal cost, c^*. The foreign firm is cost-efficient in the sense that it can produce the good at a lower cost when compared to the home firm. To capture this we assume

$$c^r = c^* \tag{10.7}$$

so that, given constant marginal costs, the total cost of producing the good for the home firm always exceeds that for the foreign firm for a given level of output. In the presence of a hire-and-fire policy, the home firm's cost inefficiency is reflected in higher MC as well. Condition (10.7) has far-reaching implications for the price strategy of the foreign firm as we will see shortly. In fact, different assumptions regarding c^r and c^*, consistent with the requirement that the home firm is cost inefficient, may produce different outcomes. However, we abstract from these variations and confine ourselves to the cases implied by eqn. (10.7). The foreign firm has no capacity constraint. Entry and transport costs are assumed to be zero. Thus, when the domestic economy is opened up, the foreign firm enters and competes with the high cost, capacity-constrained home firm.

Regarding the strategies, we assume that the home firm chooses an output level within its capacity, and the efficient foreign entrant chooses a price: accommodating or predatory. In the former case the foreign entrant sets a price which maximizes its profit given the incumbent's choice of output. Of course, even in that case the home firm may withdraw itself from the market if it makes losses—a possibility that may be called "natural" predation. Thus, under the accommodating strategy, the foreign firm sets the price according to the following rule:

$$\begin{matrix} max \\ p \end{matrix} \cdot (p - c^*)\left[D(p) - x\right] = \begin{matrix} max \\ x^* \end{matrix} \cdot x^* (a - c^* - x - x^*) \qquad (10.8)$$

On the other hand, under the predatory strategy the foreign firm charges a price just below the home MC,

$$p_P = c - \in \qquad (10.9)$$

and earns a profit π^*_p by capturing the entire market. Such a predatory profit can be calculated as, for $\in$ sufficiently close to zero,

$$\Pi^* P = (a - c)(c - c^*) \qquad (10.10)$$

Thus, when a foreign entrant predates, the home incumbent stops production. On the other hand, when a foreign firm accommodates, the best it can do is to produce up to capacity. Since, by our assumption the home firm is a "price taker", at a constant MC, it is always optimal for it to produce at full capacity at any price chosen by entrant above its MC. Indeed, as we have already pointed out, even in that case it may withdraw itself from the market. Therefore, the home incumbent either produces the capacity output or produces nothing. If the foreign firm adopts an accommodating strategy the following solutions can be obtained:

$$p = (a + c + 2c^*) / 4 \qquad (10.11)$$

$$\Pi^* = (a + c - 2c^*)^2 / 16 \qquad (10.12)$$

$$\Pi = (a - c^*)(a - 3c + 2c^*) / 8 \qquad (10.13)$$

The equilibrium is illustrated in Figure 10.1. Given the home firm's capacity output the foreign entrant faces the residual demand as indicated by the curve passing through point 'a' labelled $D_R D'_R$. The entrant sets the price by equating its MC with the marginal revenue at this residual demand. Such a price is shown to be Op along with the entrant's output Ox^* and total output $pb = Ox^* + \bar{x}$. The incumbent and the entrant enjoy profits equal to the area $pca'd$ (or $pdac''$) and area $pfec^*$ respectively.

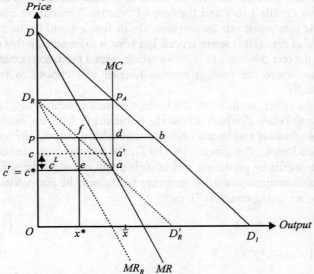

Fig. 10.1   Post-liberalization duopoly equilibrium.

However, of these alternatives, namely, duopoly, natural predation and strategic predation, which one will be the actual post-liberalization equilibrium depends not only on the degree of cost asymmetry of firms but also on the applicability of the exit or hire-and-fire policy. We now turn to this.

10.4   Post-Liberalization Market Structure in the Absence of an Exit Policy: The Case of Sunk Labour Costs

Suppose the home firm cannot employ the hire-and-fire policy so that labour costs are not variable costs but "sunk" costs :

$$S = c^L . \bar{x} \tag{10.14}$$

which cannot be avoided by stopping production. Under such circumstances, the home firm will "shut down" only if losses from producing the capacity output are equal to, or greater than, the sunk cost, S. But this happens to be the case when,

$$p < MC = c^r$$

which is essentially the predatory price. Therefore, as long as the foreign firm accommodates, the home firm does not stop production even if it entails a loss and the case of "natural" predation does not arise. At this point our assumption about foreign and home MC as indicated in eqn. (10.7) seems crucial. But what is to be noted is that even if $c^r > c^*$, the cost difference $(c^r - c^*)$ for which natural predation occurs is the situation where the foreign entrant himself will choose to predate strategically.

On the other hand, when the foreign entrant predates, i.e., charges a price just below c^r which is now the home firm's MC, the home firm stops production and incurs only the sunk labour costs, S, in order to minimize losses.[2] But given eqn. (10.7), the foreign firm cannot earn positive profits by predating and as such it will never predate. That is, the post-liberalization market structure will always be duopolistic with solution set, using eqn. (10.7), as:[3]

$$p = (a + 3c^*) / 4 \tag{10.15}$$

$$\Pi = (a - c^*)^2 / 8 - S \tag{10.16}$$

$$\Pi^* = (a - c^*)^2 / 16 \tag{10.17}$$

$$W = 13(a - c^*)^2 / 32 - S \tag{10.18}$$

It should be noted that given eqn. (10.7), the absence of an exit policy effectively makes the home and foreign firms equally efficient in terms of MCs. As labour costs are now sunk, they do not affect output and price levels, and overall cost asymmetry can in no way affect the post-liberalization equilibrium. Hence,

Proposition 1: In the absence of a hire-and-fire policy, the foreign entrant will always accommodate and post-liberalization market structure will always be duopolistic, provided eqn. (10.7) holds.

For gains from liberalization, on the other hand, we must compare W in eqn. (10.18) with autarkic welfare in the absence of an exit policy which is given as

$$W_A = [3(a - c^*)^2 / 8] - S \qquad (10.19)$$

It can be easily verified that, $W > W_A$ so that we have positive gains from liberalization. Thus, the absence of an exit or hire-and-fire policy does not stand in the way of these gains.

10.4.1 Post-liberalization market structure under exit policy: case of variable labour cost

Here we assume that the home firm can apply the hire-and-fire policy, i.e., can lay-off workers whenever required. The labour costs are, therefore, variable and the home firm's MC is $c^r + c^L$. Contrary to the previous case, the home firm will stop production whenever it faces any losses. On the other hand, as the home firm is now inefficient in terms of MC also, the foreign entrant can earn positive profit under the predatory strategy. This means that the monopoly of the foreign firm is also a probable result in the post-liberalization market structure. However, since there is no entry or exit cost, the foreign firm cannot fully exercise its monopoly power by charging the monopoly price, $p^*_m = (a + c^*)/2$, when the home incumbent stops production due to the possibility of a "hit-and-run (re-) entry" by the home incumbent.[4]

Thus, the foreign firm can either charge an accommodating price, earning a profit π^* given in eqn. (10.12), or can earn predatory profit π^*_p as given in eqn. (10.10). Comparing these profit levels we observe that,

$$\Pi^* \gtreqless \Pi^*_P \quad \text{as} \quad c \lesseqgtr c_1 = .08a + .92c^* \qquad (10.20)$$

Therefore, the foreign firm accommodates when the home incumbent is not too inefficient as shown above; for higher cost differences it predates and domestic production ceases altogether. That is,

Proposition 2:   The post-entry optimal strategy of the foreign entrant depends upon the degree of cost asymmetry. When the home incumbent is not too inefficient, the foreign entrant prefers to accommodate and the post-liberalization market structure is duopolistic ; otherwise, the entrant predates and the home incumbent stops production.

Corollary 1:   The larger the domestic market, the greater is the range of cost difference for which the efficient entrant accommodates as is evident from eqn. (10.20).

This means that, *ceteris paribus*, countries with a different domestic market size will have different post-liberalization experiences regarding the nature of firm strategy and domestic production.

The post-liberalization welfare under exit policy, on the other hand, can be calculated as

$$W = \begin{cases} [(3a-c-2c^*)(3a+c-4c^*)+ \\ \qquad 4(a-c^*)(a-3c+2c^*)]/32 \quad \forall c < c_1 \\ (a-c)^2/2 = W_P \qquad \qquad \qquad \forall c > c_1 \end{cases} \quad (10.21)$$

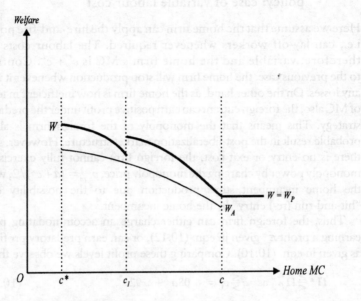

Fig. 10.2   Gains from liberalization under exit policy.

Comparing this welfare level with that under autarky as given in eqn. (10.6) we observe that

$$W > W_A \quad \forall \; c \qquad \qquad (10.22)$$

Thus, once again gains from liberalization are positive, and this result is independent of the strategy choice of the efficient foreign entrant contrary to our previous findings (Acharyya and Marjit 1997). The welfare result is illustrated in Figure 10.2 where the bold discontinuous line represents the post-liberalization welfare level under varying degrees of cost asymmetry. That gains from liberalization is positive for $c > c_1$ follows from the fact that the post-liberalization price is the predatory price, i.e., equals the (home) MC, which is "efficient". For lower cost differences we have a duopoly situation with higher total and domestic output and lower price compared to those in the pre-liberalized state. Thus, the consumers' surplus increases, while the home firm's profit may rise or fall. On the whole, however, total surplus or welfare is found to increase. But, as can be noticed from Figure 10.2, if duopolistic equilibrium holds for a greater cost range than $(c^* . c_1)$, post-liberalization welfare (under duopoly) is not necessarily higher than autarkic welfare.

10.5   Conclusions

We have examined the nature of post-liberalization equilibrium and the gains from liberalization result in terms of a two-stage game between cost asymmetric home and foreign firms. In the presence of a hire-and-fire or exit policy, the post-liberalization equilibrium crucially depends on the degree of cost asymmetry. The home incumbent produces the capacity output when it is not too inefficient or the domestic market size is not too small. Otherwise, the efficient foreign entrant predates and we have a monopoly situation. However, in any case the gains are positive, though the magnitude of such gains varies with the degree of cost asymmetry.

On the other hand, in the absence of an exit policy, the inefficient home incumbent cannot avoid the labour costs by stopping production, i.e., labour costs are "sunk" and the interesting observation is that the chances of predation as the optimal strategy of the foreign entrant is now lower than in the presence of an exit policy.[5] The absence of an exit policy, therefore, does not obstruct gain from liberalization nor does it put the home firm in a disadvantageous position *vis-à-vis* the foreign rival.

The above analysis can be extended in several directions. One such extension is to consider tariff as an alternative regime. Also, the incorporation of technology licensing may alter the post-liberalization game.

Notes

1.   In India, the existing legal provisions require the prior permission of the government for lay-off and closures of establishments employing 100 or more workers (Industrial Disputes Act, 1982). This state of affairs is described as absence of an "exit" policy.

2.   At this point, we set aside the issue of financing such losses.

3.   Once again our assumption that $c^r = c*$ seems crucial.
     If $c^r > c*$, the foreign firm may predate depending on the cost difference, $c^r - c*$.

4.   Indeed, if we consider a very flexible time structure that allows the foreign firm to respond to the incumbent's strategy quickly enough, such a hit-and-run entry possibility may be ruled out and the foreign firm may earn the monopoly profit $\Pi^*_m = (a + c*)^2/4$ (see Tirole 1988, 310).

5.   The chances of predation are lower since, due to the sunk costs, the foreign entrant can capture the entire market only by lowering price to such an extent that home firm's losses exceed its sunk costs. That is, due to sunk costs the home firm 'precommits', which is credible, and this makes predation a less attractive strategy for the entrant than in the absence of any sunk cost. In the entry literature, precommitment by the incumbent usually ap~~ars as an entry deterrent strategy. But here it affects the post-entry strategy choice of the entrant. See, for example, Dixit (1980), Gilbert (1986) and Ware (1984).

References

Acharyya, R. (1995). Theoretical aspects of liberal trade policies in transition economies: exchange rate, competition and exports. Ph.D. dissertation, Jadavpur University.

Acharyya, R. and S. Marjit. (1997). To liberalize or not to liberalize an LDC market with an inefficient incumbent. *International Review of Economics and Finance*.

Benoit, J.P. and V. Krishna. (1987). Dynamic duopoly: Prices and quantities. *Review of Economic Studies* LIV: 23–35.

Dixit, A. (1980). The role of investment in entry deterrence. *Economic Journal* 90: 95–106.

Gilbert, R.J. (1986). Preemptive competition. In *New Developments in the Analysis of Market Structure*, ed. J.E. Stiglitz and G.E. Mathewson. London: Macmillan.

Kabiraj, T. (1994). Free trade vs. autarky : A welfare analysis. *The Indian Economic Journal* 41, 3.

Kreps, D.M. and J.A. Scheinkman. (1983). Cournot precommitment and Bertrand competition yields Cournot outcome. *Bell Journal of Economics* 14: 326–37.

Rasmusen, E. (1990). *Games and Information: An Introduction to Game Theory*. Oxford: Basil Blackwell.

Tirole, J. (1988). *The Theory of Industrial Organization*. Boston, MA: MIT Press.

Ware, R. (1984). Sunk cost and strategic commitment: A proposed three stage equilibrium. *Economic Journal* 94: 370–378.